BANDS

Steve McLean

TRICKLE
ROCK
BOOKS

© 2005 by Trickle Rock Books Inc.
First printed in 2005 10 9 8 7 6 5 4 3 2 1
Printed in Canada

The Publisher: Trickle Rock Books Inc.

Library and Archives Canada Cataloguing in Publication

McLean, Steve, 1966–
  Hot Canadian bands / Steve McLean.

Includes bibliographical references.
ISBN-13: 978-1-894864-53-4
ISBN-10: 1-894864-53-0

  1. Rock groups—Canada. I. Title. II. Series.

ML394.M163 2006   781.66'092271   C2006-901007-2

Cover Image: Simple Plan, courtesy of image.net
Photography credits: Every effort has been made to accurately credit the sources of photographs. Any errors or omissions should be directed to the publisher for changes in future editions. Photographs courtesy of Dustin Rabin (p. 127; p. 129; p. 131; p. 132; p. 154); image.net (title page; p. 65; p. 67; p. 68; p. 71; p. 72; p. 113; p. 116-117; p. 145; p. 152); Jeffrey Remedios (p. 135; p. 155); www.umusicbiz.ca (p. 28; p. 34; p. 85; p. 86; p. 90; p. 149); Chapman Baehler (p. 37; p. 42; p. 47; p. 49; p. 51; p. 52; p. 143; p. 144); Chris Smith (p. 121; p. 124; p. 153); Chris Grismer (p. 5; p. 27; p. 32-33; p. 142); Steven Dewall (p. 93; p. 96-97; p. 100; p. 150); Marina Chavez (p. 9; p. 11; p. 14-15; p. 140); Emily Shur (p. 19; p. 141); Hilary Leftik (p. 75; p. 79; p. 83; p. 148); Richard Beland (p. 55; p. 57; p. 59; p. 61; p. 62; p. 147); Andrew McNaughton (p. 102; p. 106; p. 109; p. 151)

PC: P5

contents

Dedication

This book is dedicated to my mom, Joan McLean. You're my rock. You've always been there for me and you always will be. I love you.

Acknowledgements

Thank you to all of the artists who took the time to talk to me for this book. Thanks to all of the record company and independent publicists for their assistance in setting up interviews and providing me with information and music. Thanks to all of the writers and journalists who talked to and wrote about the artists in this book before I did. And thanks to Rachelle for urging me to write this book, co-signing my contract and taking my publicity photo. My apologies to everyone who I didn't get to spend enough time with while I was writing this. I'll try to make up for it.

introduction

When I sat down to write this book, I wanted to profile 10 to 15 of Canada's hottest rock bands. That may not sound like too tough a job, but even though I've been making a living from writing about the Canadian music industry for more than 14 years, it was. The reason is simple: there have never been as many hot Canadian bands as there are today.

My initial list was made up of 30 groups—at least twice as many as needed. After a lot of thinking about various factors and consulting with people whose opinions I respect, I got my final choices down to the 15 bands in the pages to come. I considered a number of elements in the whittling process, including sales, radio and video play, live appeal, critical acclaim, geographical and label diversity, future potential, album currency, and my own personal taste. I also wanted to cover a broad spectrum of rock styles.

You'll find fewer fickle animals than 21st century music fans—what people love one year may be forgotten the next. I also know that arguments can be made for some groups that were left out of this book. Heck, there are a lot of acts I love that didn't make the cut. But I'm satisfied with with the mix and feel that it represents a strong cross-section of Canadian bands that have a lot to offer the world.

There's the heavy "screamo" rock of Alexisonfire from St. Catharines, Ontario. Montreal's Arcade Fire has become one of the most talked-about bands in North America and Europe, partly because of its use of non-traditional rock instruments to create a rich and powerful orchestral sound. Toronto's Broken Social Scene has a fluctuating lineup because of the busy schedules of its members, many of whom have successful musical projects of their own. But everything somehow holds together, and the results can often be transcendent. Victoria's Hot Hot Heat recalls the energy and melodic quirkiness of early '80s new wave groups. Matt Mays and El Torpedo could become the next Neil Young and Crazy Horse or Tom Petty and the Heartbreakers—not bad for a group of self-admitted hosers from Dartmouth, Nova Scotia.

Emily Haines, frontwoman for the cosmopolitan Metric, has become a sex symbol without sacrificing musical or personal credibility. Vancouver's The New Pornographers are creating some of the best power pop tunes that you'll hear anywhere. Nickelback emerged from tiny Hanna, Alberta, to make music that's tailor-made for both rock radio and pyrotechnic-filled arena concerts. Simple Plan has ridden the pop-punk wave from Montreal clubs to international stardom. The Tragically Hip has been making great music for more than 20 years since the band first formed in Kingston, Ontario, and has gained a following as loyal as any you'll ever see.

I could go on, but I think you get the picture. There's no shortage of great Canadian music. And in the last couple of years, the rest of the world has started to pay more attention. Although new technology has helped make it easier and more economical to record, distribute and promote music, none of that matters unless you have talent.

The 15 bands that you're about to read about all have talent. You may not be a fan of all of them, but they all have stories that—like their music—deserve to be heard.

nickelback

The members of Nickelback were The Village Idiots when they were playing other people's songs in the small town of Hanna, Alberta. But they've since proven themselves to be some of the most astute and successful musicians that Canada has ever produced.

Mike Kroeger moved from Hanna to Vancouver, where he played bass in a heavy metal band and served coffee at Starbucks, often giving customers five cents change—which is where the name Nickelback came from. Mike's singer and guitarist brother Chad borrowed $4000 so that he could go to Vancouver with guitarist Ryan Peake. Along with the brothers' cousin Brandon Kroeger, they recorded a seven-song EP titled *Hesher*. When the band began getting airplay on Vancouver rock station CFOX, Chad Kroeger and Peake moved to Vancouver for good.

Nickelback recorded its debut independent album, *Curb*, with producer Larry Anschell in December 1996. "Fly" became the most played song on CFOX, and three tracks from the album were featured in EA Sports' *Triple Play 99 Baseball* video game.

While *Curb* made Nickelback one of the most popular bands in Vancouver, it was the group's 1999 independent album *The State* that raised its profile across Canada. Produced by the group and Dale Penner (Holly McNarland, Matthew Good Band, Econoline Crush) and mixed by GGGarth Richardson (Rage Against The Machine, 54.40), the disc featured new drummer Ryan Vikedal, a friend of Peake's from Brooks, Alberta. "Leader of Men" was a hit, and Nickelback traversed the country in support of the record.

Ralph James at the Agency Group booked Nickelback's shows, but the band members were handling management, radio promotion, marketing and distribution of the album themselves. They did it so well that *The State* sold 10,000 copies within a few months, and the group began attracting the attention of record companies.

"I'm just as much a businessman as I am a musician," said Chad in a February 3, 2000 article in the *Calgary Sun*. "I sold advertising for a soccer magazine for a couple of years, and it was the exact same thing. When I got [our songs] on the radio and in rotation, it was just like making a sale. I loved it."

When the business end of things became too big for the musicians to handle on their own, the band signed deals with EMI Music Canada for its homeland and Roadrunner Records for the rest of the world. *The State* was re-released, and Nickelback spent most of 1999 and 2000 touring Canada and the U.S., where "Leader of Men" became a top-10 rock radio hit.

2005

BaNd tRiViA

Chad Kroeger spent two months in a juvenile detention centre when he was 14 after breaking in to his junior high school 11 times.

"A lot of people say we sort of sound American," Chad said in an article in the December 9, 1999 issue of the *Ottawa Citizen*. "If you're singing about Canadian history and Canadian stories, what patriotic, flag-waving Yank is going to want to hear about that?"

Nickelback wasn't forgotten at home, however, as it was named best new group at the 2001 Juno Awards, and *The State* went on to sell more than 100,000 copies. But that paled in comparison to what came next.

"How You Remind Me," the first single from Nickelback's *Silver Side Up* album, was released in August 2001. It became the first single by a Canadian band to top the American and Canadian charts simultaneously since The Guess Who's "American Woman" in 1970 and was the most played song on U.S. radio in 2002. Peake thinks that the song's subject matter was one of the keys to its success.

"I mean, at some point everybody has had a sh**ty relationship. They hear the song and they're like, 'I know exactly what you mean.' People like having their story told. I think that's what it is," he said in a January 31, 2002 article in the *Ottawa Citizen*.

Silver Side Up was recorded at Vancouver's Greenhouse Studios, produced by Rick Parashar (Pearl Jam, Temple of the Dog) and mixed at Vancouver's Armoury Studios by Randy Staub (Metallica, U2). The album broadened the group's sound considerably.

Some parts were lighter and more melodic than on previous albums, while in other places on the disc the band was heavier and more aggressive than it had ever been.

Silver Side Up was released on that fateful day, September 11, 2001, and debuted at number one on the Canadian sales chart and at number two in the U.S. The singles "Too Bad" and "Never Again" followed "How You Remind Me" up the radio charts and ensured strong sales for the album.

"Gone are the ideas of re-inventing the wheel or starting a revolution," said Mike of Nickelback's popularist approach to making music in an article in the January 15, 2002 issue of the *Victoria Times Colonist*. "We're just making our version of hard rock music."

Staub won the 2002 Juno for best recording engineer for "How You Remind Me" and "Too Bad," while "How You Remind Me" was named best single. *Silver Side Up* was crowned best rock album, and Nickelback took the best group prize at the awards

ceremony in St. John's, Newfoundland. "Too Bad" was chosen as best video and best rock video at the 2002 MuchMusic Video Awards. *Silver Side Up* has sold more than 10 million copies around the world and was certified octuple platinum in Canada, quintuple platinum in the U.S., triple platinum in the UK, double platinum in Australia and platinum in Germany.

> "We never had this idea where we're going to play on these awards shows and festivals in places like Australia," said Peake in an article in the January 25, 2004 edition of the *Edmonton Sun*. "I don't think my brain at the time could conceive of those kind of things. We went on small goals, not large ones. And that, I think, kept us real."

Curb was re-released on August 6, 2002, to appease fans who wanted to hear what Nickelback sounded like in its early days. A January 25, 2002 concert in Edmonton was recorded and released on DVD (along with the videos for "How You Remind Me," "Too Bad" and "Leader Of Men" and a documentary on the making of the "Too Bad" clip) in December 2002.

Chad and Josey Scott (Saliva) recorded the song "Hero" for the successful *Spider-Man* soundtrack. It topped the rock charts in the summer of 2002 and helped earn Chad and Nickelback the 2003 Juno for songwriter of the year.

Chad recorded a song called "Why Don't You and I" with Carlos Santana for the veteran guitarist's 2002 hit album, *Shaman*. Nickelback, Kid Rock and guitarist Dimebag Darrell Abbott (Pantera) teamed up to record a cover of Elton John's "Saturday Night's Alright For Fighting" for the soundtrack of the 2003 film, *Charlie's Angels: Full Throttle*.

Chad again combined his music and business knowledge when he formed his own label, 604 Records, with lawyer Jonathan Simkin in 2002. The company has released albums from Theory Of A Deadman, Thornley, Tommy Lee, The Organ, Armchair Cynics, Marianas Trench, The Solution and Tin Foil Phoenix.

With help from engineer Joey Moi, Nickelback produced the band's fourth album at Greenhouse and Chad's home studio, Mountainview Studios. Staub once again did the mixing. The Long Road was released in September 2003 and debuted at number one on the Canadian sales chart after selling more than 45,000 copies in its first week. The CD entered the sales chart at number three in New Zealand, number four in Australia and Germany, number five in the UK and number six in the U.S.

Nickelback embarked on the largest and most successful Canadian tour ever produced by any group, in support of *The Long Road*. The band and a crew of 35 people traveled from coast to coast, playing 43 concerts that showcased a pyrotechnic display that reportedly cost $150,000 a week. "If we don't have any explosions during one song, we make up for it in the next," said Peake in an article in the February 12, 2004 issue of *Nightlife*.

Driven by the singles "Someday," "Figured You Out" and "Feelin' Way Too Damn Good," *The Long Road* went on to sell more than 400,000 copies in Canada and more than five million around the world. The album helped Nickelback win the group of the year and fan choice titles at the 2004 Juno Awards in Edmonton.

A DVD titled *The Videos* featuring seven Nickelback videos was released in September 2003. It was reissued with bonus documentary footage on the making of *The Long Road* in November 2004.

Before Nickelback started recording its next album, Vikedal was let go during a January 3, 2005 meeting at the house of the band's tour

Nickelback (L to R): Mike Kroeger, Daniel Adair, Ryan Peake, Chad Kroeger (2005)

manager. "I feel pretty betrayed by what was once called a family," Vikedal said in a January 28, 2005 article in the *Edmonton Sun*.

"It was hard to say goodbye," said Peake of Vikedal's departure in an article in the October 2005 issue of *Chart*. "He's a really good friend of mine. One of those business group decisions you have to make and hopefully people will understand."

> The plot thickened when Chad and his Arm Your Dillo Publishing Inc. production company sued Vikedal in November 2005, claiming damages for royalty payments Vikedal received since he was fired from the group.

Vikedal was replaced by former 3 Doors Down drummer Daniel Adair, who the band members felt could bring a heavier sound to the group. Nickelback spent seven months recording the album with Moi at Mountainview, and Staub mixed it at Vancouver's Warehouse Studios. Guest guitarists Billy Gibbons (ZZ Top) and Dimebag Darrell Abbott (Pantera) contributed to the album.

"On *The Long Road* we went in a heavier direction, but with this album we really wanted to show our range and have songs that work for all the diverse fans that go to Nickelback shows and listen to our records," says Chad.

Lead single and video "Photograph" was a strong introduction to *All the Right Reasons*, which was released in October 2005. The album sold more than 60,000 copies in Canada and more than 324,000 in the U.S. in its first week, landing it at the top of the sales charts in both countries. The disc was certified double platinum in Canada within two weeks of its release and quadruple platinum in the U.S. by the end of the year. Nickelback launched a cross-Canada tour in support of the album in early 2006.

"I want to be that guy who gets played on classic-rock radio stations 20 years down the road," said Chad in an article in the February 5, 2004 issue of the *Toronto Star*. "Who doesn't want that? Who wants to be part of a fad or a trend where your music becomes popular and you're part of a 'where are they now?' special 10 years down the road. Who doesn't want to have a piece of history?"

After selling 17 million records around the globe in its still relatively young career, Nickelback's place in rock music history seems assured.

sum 41

Sum 41 was formed in Ajax, Ontario, in 1996, 41 days into the summer break before the band members entered grade 12.

"We grew up in a boring small town where there wasn't much to do, so we went skateboarding and listened to music," says singer, songwriter and guitarist Deryck Whibley. "And after listening to that type of music, we started to play it ourselves."

Whibley, Dave Baksh (guitar), Jason "Cone" McCaslin (bass) and Steve Jocz (drums) played enough of their pop-punk metal-based music to attract the attention of EMI Music Publishing Canada president Michael McCarty, who watched the band play in a basement. "We were really bad at the time, but he must have seen something in us that made him decide to take a chance and get involved with us, and they were really supportive," says Whibley.

Sum 41 used money from EMI to make an electronic press kit that included footage of the band's high-energy live performances and clips of the boys' drive-by assaults with industrial-sized squirt guns. The kit was sent to record companies while the group was shopping for a deal, and Montreal's Aquarius Records was the first to show an interest. Island Records, a division of the powerhouse Universal Music Group, came on board a short time later. But the quartet wanted to show its appreciation to Aquarius and signed to the independent label in Canada while Island acquired the international rights.

Singer and guitarist Greig Nori (Treble Charger), who went on to produce three of Sum 41's first four albums, managed the band and later became involved with Nettwerk Management as the group became more successful. "We treat him like a fifth member of the band," Whibley says.

Sum 41's *Half Hour of Power* debut album features metal and punk elements with a bit of rap on "It's What We're All About" and some ska on "Second Chance For Max Headroom." The record spawned the pop-punk single "Makes No Difference," which helped carry *Half Hour of Power* to gold certification in Canada for selling 50,000 copies.

Sum 41 toured heavily in support of the debut and developed a growing fan base that helped set the stage for the group's major breakthrough, 2001's *All Killer No Filler* album. Jerry Finn, who

Sum 41 (L to R): Jason "Cone" McCaslin, Dave Baksh, Deryck Whibley, Steve Jocz (2005)

has also worked with Green Day, Blink-182 and Fenix, TX, produced the disc. It features the hits "Motivation," "Handle This," the poppier "In Too Deep" and the anti-conformist "Fat Lip," which mixes a bit of rap with heavy guitar rock and extols the band members' fondness for Iron Maiden and Judas Priest.

The video for "Fat Lip" features the band pretending to be a fictitious spandex-clad metal group called Pain For Pleasure, while the "In Too Deep" clip shows Whibley doing a fancy high dive. Both of the videos helped broaden Sum 41's exposure considerably when they were aired heavily on music television channels around the world.

The group also circumnavigated the globe to take its extravagant live show (which included playing on top of a mountain of skulls) to its many new fans, who are affectionately known as "goons"—a label that the band members had previously fixed on themselves.

All Killer No Filler was certified triple platinum in Canada, double platinum in the U.S. and the UK, platinum in Ireland and Japan, and gold in France, Indonesia and Australia.

In 2002, Sum 41 released *Introduction to Destruction*, a DVD featuring the band's September 28, 2001 performance at the Astoria in London, England, all of the group's music videos, commentary, five short feature films, five home movies, exclusive photos and a link to a special Sum 41 website. It was followed shortly thereafter by the band's third album, *Does This Look Infected?*

The record continued the style of the earlier releases and, like those albums, clocked in at well under 40 minutes. Whibley, who has suffered through bouts of writer's block, comes up with

BaNd tRiViA

The band members like using nicknames for themselves. Deryck Whibley has been known as Bizzy D, Sir Biznatch and Biz. Dave Baksh has been credited as Hot Chocolate, Brown Sound, The Right Honorable Sir Captain David Brownsound Of The First Airborne Regiment Heavyweight Champion Ph.D. and Dave Brownsound. Steve Jocz has been listed on albums as Stevo 32, Stevo Dirty Poo and just plain old Stevo. Jason McCaslin more often goes by the name Cone.

relatively short songs and doesn't produce any more than he feels he has to.

"I don't write with anyone else but myself in mind," he asserts. "Every song that I've ever written has appeared on our albums. We're not the kind of band that will write 30 songs and then pick the best 12 to record. We write 12 songs and that's what we record."

Does This Look Infected? features the hits "Still Waiting," "Over My Head (Better Off Dead)" and "The Hell Song," an unusually serious song for Whibley, written about a friend who was diagnosed with HIV. The song's video, however, showed that Sum 41 hadn't lost its knack for coming up with humorous visual concepts. The clip features toy action figures of the band with doll versions of George Bush, Snoop Dogg, Ozzy and Sharon Osbourne and members of Korn, KISS, AC/DC and Destiny's Child.

Does This Look Infected? also included DVD content titled *Cross the T's and Gouge Your I's* that featured the songs "Reign in Pain (Heavy Metal Jamboree)" and "WWVII Part Two" as well as clips of the band goofing around—including brief snippets of nudity that drew the ire of the Manitoba Film Classification Board and earned the DVD an R rating.

"Manitoba got mad at us and now kids have to get IDed when they buy the CD and, if they're not 18, they take the DVD away," complained Baksh in a November 26, 2002 ChartAttack.com article. "They have to get their older brother or some bum to buy it for them."

There were no such problems with *Sake Bombs and Happy Endings: Live in Tokyo*, a DVD that captured the band's 20-song performance at the Bay NK Hall on May 17, 2003, which was released later that year.

Sum 41 was named group of the year at the 2003 Juno Awards and *Does This Look Infected?* was certified platinum in Canada. But the band remained active on the international front, touring the world and earning a platinum certification in Japan and gold records in the U.S., the UK, France, Indonesia and Australia.

Sum 41 traveled to the eastern region of the Democratic Republic of Congo for 10 days in May 2004 with War Child, a Canadian charity that provides humanitarian assistance to children affected by war. They shot a documentary, *Rocked: Sum 41 in the Congo* (which was released on DVD in November 2005), to help expose the devastating impact of the country's longstanding civil war that had killed more than three million people in the previous six years.

> In the conflict zone, the group members got caught in the crossfire between government soldiers and troops loyal to a renegade commander. "We went to Congo to show people what war is like, how harmful it is to civilians, and we ended up becoming war-affected ourselves," says Jocz.

Sum 41 was evacuated from Congo with the help of Canadian peacekeeper Chuck Pelletier, and the group's 2004 *Chuck* release was named in his honor. While Whibley claimed that the Congo experience had a minimal effect on his music, many journalists thought differently after listening to the album.

"This record is a little more serious, I guess, and it's like we've evolved a little bit," said Whibley in an October 12, 2004 MTV.com article. "But we were heading in that direction with our last record anyway. I mean, in every single interview, people ask us why this is our 'serious record,' which is really surprising because there are, like, two songs that are maybe sort of serious."

One of those songs was the first single, "We're All to Blame," which criticizes the greed, ignorance and fear-mongering that's rife in North American society. But, as with "The Hell Song," the light-hearted video for the track juxtaposed its somewhat somber message. The clip pays warped tribute to the cheesy 1980s television music show *Solid Gold* and its infamous dancers.

Cello, piano and acoustic guitar were introduced to some songs on *Chuck*, but the album also included cuts like the Anthrax and Metallica-influenced "The Bitter End." The group was clearly expanding its horizons by embracing both ends of the soft-loud spectrum and could no longer be as easily pigeonholed by critics as it was in the early days. "We consider ourselves a rock band, and there's so much music that we like that falls under that category that we don't see ourselves as any certain style of rock band," Whibley emphasizes.

Chuck also spun off the singles "Some Say," "No Reason" and "Pieces," a number one rock radio hit in Canada. It took the 2005 Juno for best rock album and was certified double platinum in Canada, platinum in Japan and gold in the U.S. and Indonesia.

If Sum 41's members seemed to be maturing on their records, they weren't necessarily doing the same offstage or at their shows.

Stories about the group smashing up hotel rooms, vomiting on other artists, being thrown out of bars and pulling all sorts of pranks have followed the band throughout its career. The group also drew criticism from some parents and journalists for showing a violent film clip that shows Jocz brutally murdering McCaslin as part of the stage show during its 2004–05 tour.

> "We're just being ourselves" is Whibley's response to those who say that Sum 41 is a poor role model for younger fans. "You can either like us for being us, or don't like us. It doesn't make any difference because there are millions of other people who buy our records. We're not a kids band, and we don't consider ourselves a family act. If parents want to bring their kids to shows and are cool with it, that's fine. But we're not going to change what we are because of that."

Sum 41's profile has also received a major boost through its contributions to other projects. "What We're All About" was included on 2002's mega-selling *Spider-Man* soundtrack. The band covered Canadian metal pioneer Helix's "Rock You" on the soundtrack to the 2002 *Spinal Tap*-like Canadian film, *FUBAR*. The group collaborated with punk godfather Iggy Pop on his 2003 single "Little Know It All." It recorded a song called "Moron" for Fat Wreckchords' 2004 *Rock Against Bush* package. Sum 41 contributed "Noots" (which was previously only released as a bonus track on the Australian and Japanese versions of *Chuck*) to the *Fantastic Four* movie and soundtrack in 2005. The same year, it performed the title song on the *Killer Queen: A Tribute* compilation and participated in the all-star UNICEF charity single, "Do They Know It's Halloween?" The quartet was also part of Amnesty International's "Make Some Noise" program, where artists covered John Lennon songs to raise awareness and funds for the charity's human rights work.

"Those things come up because we get asked to do them," says Whibley. "We've never gone after any of them—and we turn down a lot of stuff."

An animated version of Sum 41 guest-starred in an episode of the TV comedy *King of the Hill*, and the real-life group was featured in the 2005 documentary, *Punk's Not Dead*. The group portrayed another band in the film *Dirty Love*, and Jocz played a National Guardsman in *The L.A. Riot Spectacular*, a movie starring Snoop Dogg and Emilio Estevez.

Whibley, meanwhile, got engaged to Canadian pop starlet Avril Lavigne in June 2005 and moved to Los Angeles to live with her. He won't talk about their relationship, and he's almost as vague when asked about Sum 41's next album, which he was due to start working on in early 2006.

"It will be our best record, that's all I know," he says, succinctly.

metric

Metric may be the most international and well-traveled Canadian band around.

"Josh and Joules are from America, I'm a dual [U.S. and Canadian] citizen and was born in India, and James was born in England," singer and keyboardist Emily Haines said in the November 2005 issue of *Chart.* "He's a dual EU [European]/Canadian citizen."

Add those bloodlines to the fact that Haines and guitarist James Shaw, Metric's founding members, have lived in Montreal, New York City, London, Los Angeles and Toronto while pursuing their musical dreams, and it's no surprise that their music has a definite cosmopolitan quality.

Emily Haines is the daughter of the late avant-garde jazz musician Paul Haines, who instilled a love of music in her while she was growing up in Toronto. At the Etobicoke School of the Arts, she met Amy Millan and Kevin Drew. She later worked with them in Broken Social Scene.

Shaw was studying music in Boston, where he was friends with Torquil Campbell and Chris Seligman, who later formed Stars with Millan. Shaw then moved to New York City to further his music studies at the Julliard School for three years before he and Campbell moved back to Toronto in 1998.

Haines and Shaw met at the venerable Toronto music club, the Horseshoe Tavern, where they realized that they shared similar ideas and decided to form a musical partnership. Later that year, Shaw and Haines moved to New York, where they shared a flat with future members of the Yeah Yeah Yeahs and The Liars during their two-year stay. During this time, they started calling themselves Metric. The name was "meant to represent the difference between the imperialists and the rest of the world," Shaw said in an October 5, 2005 interview on gothamist.com.

Metric recorded several down-tempo, electronic-oriented demos that they called *Mainstream EP*. The tracks caught the attention of British record executives, and Shaw and Haines moved to London, England, in early 2000. They signed a deal with Chrysalis Records and started working with producer Stephen Hague, who was associated with records from New Order, Erasure and the Pet Shop Boys. The result of their efforts was a collection of electro-pop tunes that was supposed to be the basis of Metric's Chrysalis debut.

But Haines and Shaw complained that the songs were too commercial and didn't properly reflect their more underground tastes. They were also frustrated at how few shows they were able to land in England. By November, the Chrysalis deal had collapsed, and Metric moved back to New York to continue working on a drum-machine-driven album.

Haines and Shaw completed recording by April 2001 and found a new label, Los Angeles-based Restless Records, to release the disc. But the album, *Grow Up and Blow Away*, never made its way

into stores due to problems at Restless. However, many of the tracks from those sessions can now be found on the Internet.

"I think that's good because it forced us to move on, and it also meant that all these kids could end up getting music for free, and they really like it," says Haines of the label troubles and the fate of the early songs. "You can steal them online all you like."

Shaw has a similar perspective on how things turned out. "It's the perfect trial run," he said in the November 2005 issue of *Chart*.

2004

BaNd tRiViA

"Yeah yeah yeah, Broken Accidental Stars" is a line in the song "The List" that refers to the Yeah Yeah Yeahs, Broken Social Scene, K.C. Accidental and Stars—four groups that Metric has a close connection with.

"No one's going to judge you on it because it never got released; no one's going to review it because it never got released. No one's asking people to buy it. It's basically just using music as free promotion."

That same year, Metric released 500 copies of a five-song EP, produced by Shaw, titled *Static Anonymity*. Haines and Shaw should have released 499 and kept one for themselves. Haines says they don't have a copy and are always on the lookout for one, but short clips of the songs are available on the ilovemetric.com website.

Things took a definite positive turn when Haines and Shaw met drummer Joules Scott-Key and welcomed him into the group. Key's friend and fellow Texan Joshua Winstead was added a short time later to play bass. With a full lineup, Metric's live performances became much more dynamic.

"If you can play really great music in a room, people will come and listen to it, and then your career is controlled by your fans, as opposed to an industry that has their head up its ass," Shaw said in the fall 2005 issue of *Under The Radar*.

The quartet wanted to get a fresh start, and so they scrapped their previous recordings to start work on what would finally become their first album, *Old World Underground, Where Are You Now?* It was out with the more trip-hop-flavored songs of the past and in with a new-wave-influenced, danceable rock sound that emphasized Shaw's guitar work as much as Haines' keyboard playing.

Old World Underground was recorded in Los Angeles with producer Michael Andrews and was released in Canada on the fledgling Last Gang Records label that had just been launched by Toronto entertainment lawyer Chris Taylor. While the album eventually yielded five singles and videos ("Combat Baby," "The List," "Dead Disco," "Succexy" and "Calculation Theme"), it was far from an immediate smash. Still, momentum kept building even without the benefit of a major marketing push.

"The biggest poster we ever had was someone actually painted the cover of *Old World* on a wall in Vancouver," said Haines in an October 28, 2005 ChartAttack.com article. "I don't even think they were hired to do that; they just did. It wasn't ever shoved down people's throats. One person tells one person, and then it's four, and then it's eight, so it just moved around and caught on."

The Internet was also a key in both getting the word out about the album and in allowing people to hear some of it. Haines believes the online community has helped bands succeed, especially in Canada. "Often for more unique, unmarketable music, distribution is your main obstacle. But the Internet has allowed us all to get our music out, and it's much more democratic. If people like it, they like it. It could just be a kid playing acoustic guitar in his bedroom, but if they like it, it could be huge."

Old World Underground was released in the U.S., Europe and Japan, and Metric played everywhere it could for more than a year to support the album. The band also made a cameo appearance in French film director Olivier Assayas' 2004 junkie drama, *Clean*.

After all of that traveling, Shaw and Haines were welcomed back to Toronto in the fall of 2004. They set up a studio in the same loft space they'd occupied during their previous stay in the city. Scott-Key and Winstead made frequent trips north from their new adopted hometown of Oakland, California. Shaw took the production reins. With no need to worry about paying for expensive studio time or interference from an outside producer, the band could record its second album with minimal pressure from external sources.

"I think it's quite a bit more exploratory," said Shaw of the album, *Live It Out*, in the fall 2005 issue of *Under The Radar*. "I think that we, in knowing how to be a rock band, explored both territories of being a really hard rock band and a really soft one, a lot more than we did on *Old World*. I think there's some very aggressive moments and there's some very tender moments. Whereas on *Old World* it was sort of squashed down and didn't really hit either extreme."

Shaw attributes the change in the sound to the band members getting to know their audience and allowing that to shape the record. Metric's core audience no doubt appreciates *Live It Out*'s somewhat more aggressive lyrical approach as well. Haines takes a stand against conspicuous consumption, unjust wars, overblown terrorism fears and stereotypical gender roles.

> "As a group, we certainly don't have a slogan or anything," she says. "But we encourage people to try and break out from whatever's holding them back. It's definitely a positive message, to acknowledge what's wrong and take it over."

Live It Out, released in October 2005, was introduced by lead single "Monster Hospital." Despite references to the Bobby Fuller Four's 1966 hit "I Fought the Law" and a video based on the 1965 Roman Polanski film *Repulsion*, it's a thoroughly modern-sounding anti-war song.

Metric (L to R): Joshua Winstead, James Shaw, Emily Haines, Joules Scott-Key (2005)

Haines' manic energy at the microphone and keyboard, combined with her model-like looks, has made her somewhat of a sex symbol in the indie rock world. And though she wants to be taken seriously as a musician, it's an image that she doesn't mind accepting. "I think it's funny and flattering, and it's part of the role of being a frontperson," she says.

Metric was already on the road when *Live It Out* was released, and it continued to tour almost non-stop in support of the album. But instead of the 15-passenger Ford van the group used to travel in, the band now had the luxury of a tour bus to get from city to city and a small crew to handle all the behind-the-scenes things that the members once had to do in addition to performing. Shaw found the change disconcerting after the group had looked after all the details on previous tours.

2004

"Boredom, I think, is the killer on the road for a potentially successful indie rock band like Metric. It leads to questionable sexual encounters, unmentionable excesses and futile pursuits, chasing that elusive high that happens naturally for only 75 minutes a day when we actually play," Shaw wrote in a tour diary published in the November 6, 2005 issue of the *Toronto Star*.

When Haines and Shaw aren't on the road with Metric, they're often part of the revolving-door lineup of Toronto indie rock collective Broken Social Scene. Shaw played guitar and trumpet on parts of the band's *You Forgot It in People* album, on which Haines sang "Anthems For a Seventeen Year Old Girl" and contributed backing vocals to "Looks Just Like the Sun." The two of them also played roles on Broken Social Scene's self-titled 2005 album.

Haines was also working on a solo record of voice and piano compositions, which she expects to release in the fall of 2006.

"A lot of Metric songs are written on piano, so these other songs are just ones that aren't suited to the mood or atmosphere of what Metric is doing," she says. "They're not well-suited to a rock band."

Metric returned home from playing in France in December 2005 to learn two pieces of good news: *Old World Underground* was certified gold for selling more than 50,000 copies in Canada, and the group had landed the opening slot for two sold-out Rolling Stones concerts at New York's Madison Square Garden on January 18 and 20, 2006.

"It's been a pretty steady move forward," Haines said in a September 23, 2005 *Globe and Mail* article. "I don't feel like there's suddenly something catapulting us anywhere. It's an exciting time, but it's part of the same process we've been in for many years already."

our lady peace

Guitarist Mike Turner met University of Toronto criminology student Michael Maida after putting a classified ad in Toronto's *NOW Magazine* to find a singer for his band, As If, in 1991. The two became friends, Maida changed his name to Raine to avoid confusion with his new bandmate, and the Our Lady Peace moniker was adopted from a 1943 poem written by American Mark Van Doren.

The pair met producer Arnold Lanni, a former member of Canadian pop-rock bands Sheriff and Frozen Ghost, and laid down some demo recordings at Lanni's Arnyard Studios in Toronto. Lanni's brother Robert and partner Eric Lawrence signed Our Lady Peace to their Coalition Entertainment management company and started distributing the demos to prospective record companies.

While the music attracted attention from labels in Canada and the U.S., three top executives from Sony Music Canada were the only ones to accept an invitation to come to the group's rehearsal space to see Maida, Turner, bassist Chris Eacrett and 17-year-old drummer Jeremy Taggart perform five songs in April 1993. By September, the band was back with Lanni at Arnyard recording its debut album, *Naveed*, for Sony.

Naveed, a Middle Eastern name meaning "bearer of good news," was released in Canada in March 1994. Our Lady Peace embarked on its first tour the following month with I Mother Earth and spent much of the year crossing Canada and getting its footing as a live band. It also took time out to record a version of Neil Young's "Needle and the Damage Done" for a tribute album called *Borrowed Tunes*.

A year after *Naveed*'s Canadian release, it won a Juno Award for best album design and came out in the U.S. on Relativity Records. The album had a quick impact, driven by the incendiary modern rock hit "Starseed." Legendary duo Jimmy Page and Robert Plant and Van Halen both requested Our Lady Peace as their opening act on tour, and the group performed "Naveed" on Conan O'Brien's late-night talk show.

By September, however, musical and personal differences pushed Eacrett out of the group. He was replaced by Duncan Coutts, the band's original choice as bassist in 1992, who had decided to finish his filmmaking degree at university instead of joining the group in the beginning. "I don't want to call our old bass player Chris a weak link, but there was just something in his personality and his musical direction that was beginning to become a cancer for the rest of us," Maida told the *Toronto Sun*'s Jane Stevenson in a January 21, 1997 article.

Our Lady Peace (L to R): Steve Mazur, Raine Maida, Jeremy Taggart, Duncan Coutts (2005)

BaNd tRiViA

Duncan Coutts worked as a set dresser for the
television series *Due South* before joining the band.

Our Lady Peace ended 1995 on a high note with three CASBY (Canadian Artists Selected By You) Awards for favorite new artist, release and song from Toronto radio station CFNY. *Naveed* was released in the UK in January 1996, and the group covered The Beatles' "Tomorrow Never Knows" for the film soundtrack of *The Craft* while continuing to tour relentlessly, pushing total sales of the debut album past 500,000 units.

After considering the titles *Propeller* and *Trapeze*, Our Lady Peace released its second album, *Clumsy*, in January 1997. The album debuted at number one on the Canadian sales chart, and Our Lady Peace became only the second Canadian group after The Tragically Hip to attain the feat. The album came out in the U.S. in April, and the band played Europe for the first time in May. Next came the summer Edgefest tour that also included such top acts as Silverchair, Collective Soul, I Mother Earth and Finger Eleven. The album's title song was featured on the *I Know What You Did Last Summer* soundtrack and the video for "Superman's Dead" won MuchMusic Video Awards for favorite group and video. "Automatic Flowers" and "4 AM" joined those two songs as top-10 Canadian hits.

Our Lady Peace spent 18 months playing in support of *Clumsy*, including a sold-out Canadian arena tour and headlining dates in the U.S. and Europe. The band launched its own traveling festival, Summersault, which crossed Canada with Garbage, Crystal Method, Sloan, Eve 6 and Fuel in the summer of 1998.

At the 1998 Juno Awards, Our Lady Peace was named best group and *Clumsy* was crowned rock album of the year. A remixed version of "Starseed" was placed on the *Armageddon* soundtrack, which sold almost four million copies around the globe. All the attention helped push sales of *Clumsy* past a million in Canada and 2.5 million worldwide, making Our Lady Peace the most popular band in Canada.

The group reconvened with Lanni at Arnyard to record its third album, *Happiness Is Not a Fish That You Can Catch*, which was released in Canada and the U.S. in September 1999. It became the second straight Our Lady Peace album to enter the Canadian sales chart at number one. Early the next year, Our Lady Peace headlined an arena tour that featured the Stereophonics, Spur of the Moment, Blinker the Star and some short films created by the band. The group re-introduced the Summersault festival in August and played a series of Canadian dates with A Perfect Circle, Smashing Pumpkins, Foo Fighters, Sum 41 and others.

On the radio and video fronts, "One Man Army" and "Is Anybody Home?" became big hits, with the clip for the latter earning people's choice honors for favorite Canadian group and favorite Canadian video at the 2000 MuchMusic Video Awards. *Happiness* was certified triple platinum for selling more than 300,000 copies in Canada.

The group was recording its fourth album, which Maida co-produced with Lanni, when Taggart was mugged while walking his dog. He seriously injured his knee in the altercation, so Pearl Jam drummer and Our Lady Peace friend Matt Cameron stepped in to record "Are You Sad?" and "Right Behind You" to complete the record, *Spiritual Machines*.

The album, which was released in Canada in December 2000, was inspired by Ray Kurzweil's book, *The Age of Spiritual Machines: When Computers Exceed Human Intelligence*. Kurzweil even read some short passages from his text on the album, which was recorded more quickly and with more emphasis on capturing a live sound.

"We're very hesitant to call it a 'concept record,'" Turner said in an April 2001 interview with musictoday.com. "I would say it's a 'conceptually unified' record. It wasn't like we sat down, having read the book, and said, 'Man, we've got to write a record about this!' These were things we already had been talking about amongst ourselves, and Raine already had been writing about some of them on *Happiness*. So it was just more fuel for a fire that had already been burning."

Spiritual Machines was released in the U.S., the UK, Japan and Australia in 2001, and the band continued to tour in support of the album. During sound checks, the group came up with "Whatever," which was used as the entrance music for World Wrestling Federation star Chris Benoit and later released on the organization's *Forceable Entry* compilation disc. Five weeks after the September 11 terrorist attacks in the U.S., Our Lady Peace joined The Tragically Hip, Barenaked Ladies, Alanis Morissette and others at the awareness-raising Music Without Borders concert in Toronto—a foreshadowing of Maida's socio-politically motivated charity work that followed.

"In Repair" and "Life" became major Canadian rock radio hits, and Our Lady Peace was nominated for five Junos and eight MuchMusic Video Awards. *Spiritual Machines* sold more than 200,000 copies in Canada.

Despite the group's continuing (if diminished) commercial success, it was time to make some changes. While the band still remained close to Lanni, the members decided to record their next album with Canadian producer Bob Rock (Metallica, The Cult) at his studio in Maui, Hawaii.

During a break from recording in December 2001, Maida strengthened his already firm control over the group when Turner left the band he founded 10 years earlier over creative and musical differences. "If we hadn't made the decision to replace Mike, I don't think we'd be here right now," Maida said in a November 2002 article in *Rock Sound*.

"When you're in the middle of something and you've got a record deal, you don't want to rock the boat. But with the fifth album you get to a point where if you want to keep going you have to make a change. I don't know if Mike was born to be a guitar player. The studio was a tough place for him, and we were working too hard to make up for it—we felt like we were cheating ourselves. Four albums is way too f***ing long to put up with that. I'm sure he'll do great things, just not with six-stringed instruments."

Finding themselves without a guitarist, the remaining members sent out a call for wannabes to send in audition tapes. The band screened thousands of submissions as tapes, videos, DVDs and CDs poured in from around the world.

Our Lady Peace eventually decided to go with Detroit native Steve Mazur, who the band already knew and liked as both a person and a musician. He was invited to Maui to finish recording what would eventually become *Gravity*, an album that was more aggressive and straightforward than its predecessors.

"Leaving Toronto and holing up in a beach house in Maui was a very important step for us," explains Coutts. "We lived, ate and breathed music together away from all distractions."

In addition to going for a simpler musical approach, Rock also wanted Maida to rid his lyrics of all their ambiguities and make them easier for the average person to understand. The producer's ideas seemed to work, as *Gravity* debuted at number two in Canada and number nine in the U.S. after it was released in June 2002. The album was released in the UK, Russia and Australia later in the year. *Gravity* featured the singles and videos "Somewhere Out There" and "Innocent" and became the group's most successful U.S. album since *Clumsy*, selling more than 600,000 copies there and more than 200,000 in Canada.

Our Lady Peace contributed a cover of John Lennon's "Imagine" to the *Peace Songs* CD that was released in April 2003 to raise funds for War Child Canada, a charitable organization that Maida is involved in. That same month, the band was nominated for four Junos and took home the best rock album prize.

Two months later, at the MuchMusic Video Awards, "Innocent" was honored for its cinematography and was named best video.

Two days after the awards show, Our Lady Peace's *Live* album was released in Canada, and the U.S. release followed one week later. A DVD—featuring 20 live tracks recorded in Edmonton and Calgary, audio commentary and backstage footage—came out late in the fall.

"This whole thing is like closing the chapter on the old Our Lady Peace—not that we're abandoning the sound, but it's changing a lot with the next record," Maida said of the live releases in a July 6, 2003 interview with JAM! Music. "It's nice to have something like a live DVD and live CD to follow it and really put perspective on what we've done, but for us to move on and really look forward to the future."

That future looked rocky at times from 2003 through the first part of 2005 as Our Lady Peace tried to come up with material for its sixth studio album. During that period, the band members would get together to write and record before going their separate ways again. They eventually recorded 45 songs before deciding on 12 that they really liked.

Rock produced the album and most of the tracks that eventually made the cut were recorded at his Maui studio, but material was also recorded in Los Angeles and Toronto. Paring down the tracks to a workable number proved frustrating.

"I fired Bob Rock at one point, and I think he quit at another," says Maida. "It was a very emotional process because we were fighting to not compromise our artistic vision and bring as much artistry as possible back into our music."

Maida also spent the time between records doing work for War Child, traveling to Iraq and Sudan to help film documentaries about the suffering and poverty experienced by the people in those countries.

"Those trips have defined my life even more than my music," he says. "And you can't help but let that stuff seep into the lyrics and even the sensibilities you're trying to get out of the songwriting and the emotion we're trying to get out of the music."

Our Lady Peace performed with several other big names at the Canadian Live 8 concert to raise awareness of global poverty and pressure the G8 leaders to forgive Third World debt in Barrie, Ontario on July 2, 2005.

August 2005 saw the Canadian and U.S. release of *Healthy In Paranoid Times*, while a European release followed in September. The album debuted at number two on the Canadian sales chart. Our Lady Peace played several shows in support of the record, which spawned a pair of singles and videos, "Where Are You?" and "Angels/Losing/Sleep."

"It's the album I feel most proud of," Maida said of *Healthy In Paranoid Times* in a September 3, 2005 *Calgary Sun* article. "If I die tomorrow I'm happy to have this record represent what we were."

But after recording 45 songs for the album, Maida told *FMQB* on August 19, 2005, that the band has at least 10 good tracks that didn't make it on to *Healthy In Paranoid Times* that the members want to revisit.

"Ultimately, we can put out another record in a year, which will be amazing. I'd really like to do that because I don't want to sit on that material for too long."

After waiting more than three years for *Healthy In Paranoid Times*, Our Lady Peace fans certainly don't want the group to sit on those songs for too long either.

hot hot heat

Paul Hawley came up with the name Hot Hot Heat, and his other bandmates liked it because they thought that it captured the nature of their music in the late '90s. Since the 2002 release of the breakthrough *Make Up The Breakdown* album, the name also aptly describes the West Coast group's career.

Steve Bays and Dustin Hawthorne had been making music together in various Victoria, BC bands since they were teenagers in 1995. Hawley joined them three years later as they continued to go through different instruments, lineups and band names. By 1999, Bays was playing keyboards, Hawthorne was on the bass, Hawley was banging on the drums and Matt Marnik was singing. Marnik sang on the guitarless group's two seven-inch singles and a split album with Red Light Sting as well as the group's *Scenes One Through Thirteen* full-length debut before leaving the band. Bays then took over singing duties, and guitarist Dante DeCaro rounded out the lineup.

"Not a lot of big bands came over to the island [Vancouver Island], so we got a lot of punk bands coming through," says Hawthorne of the group's formative years in Victoria. "There was a really thriving punk community there, so I got to see a lot of cool hardcore and punk bands. That definitely helped us. And at the same time, because it was so isolated, there wasn't a scene that you had to fit into. We could feel free to do what we wanted."

Hot Hot Heat's early material was harsher and more aggressive than what followed when the band signed with Seattle's influential Sub Pop Records label, and the group's early style had a limited appeal. But OHEV Records released *Scenes One Through Thirteen* in 2003, and the Red Light Sting *Split* album was reissued in 2004 to capitalize on the name value that Hot Hot Heat had established.

The first recordings made with DeCaro were unveiled on 2002's *Knock Knock Knock* EP for Sub Pop. The EP, produced in part by Chris Walla (Death Cab for Cutie), was a campus radio favorite, earning positive reviews and setting the stage for the release of *Make Up The Breakdown* later that year.

Hot Hot Heat (L to R): Dustin Hawthorne, Luke Paquin, Paul Hawley, Steve Bays (2005)

That album, recorded in just six days with producer Jack Endino (Nirvana, Soundgarden), completed Hot Hot Heat's transformation from a noisy synth-punk band into a more melodic, yet still quirky, pop combo that drew comparisons to English new wave band XTC. Bays had a distinctive and unconventional voice, and the effervescent songs on the album (labeled by various journalists as dance-rock, art-punk or dance-punk) attracted critical raves and global attention through the singles and videos "Talk To Me, Dance With Me," "No, Not Now" and especially, "Bandages." The last song gained more notoriety when it was removed from BBC Radio One's playlist in the UK for fear that the repeated title lyric might offend some listeners in light of the war in Iraq, even though the song had no references to the Iraqi war.

Make Up The Breakdown was nominated for a best alternative album Juno Award in 2003. Hot Hot Heat made numerous appearances on prominent television shows in Canada and the U.S. while building its fan base during almost two years of nonstop touring in support of the record.

In a November 6, 2002 article on ChartAttack.com, Bays noted the change in audience response to the band's music. "The crowds have been crazy and almost every show has been sold-out. Most of the crowds are dancing and singing along. There are so many kids that know all the lyrics too."

Hot Hot Heat didn't take much of a break after coming off the road before it started working on its next album in December 2003. The band members wanted to capitalize on the ideas they had come up with while touring and wanted to capture that live energy in its new material. The guys spent their time jamming during the day and writing new songs at night until, five months later, they had 25 new songs.

The quartet secluded itself in a converted barn in Shawinigan Lake, north of Victoria, and began laying down demos of the new tracks. The group decided that it could either repeat the same style as its earlier release or experiment and grow.

"What we discovered in the process was that, while we were taking huge steps forward musically, we were also coming full circle back to the style and sound that had brought us together in the first place," says Bays.

2005

BaNd tRiViA

Guitarist Dante DeCaro, who left the band after recording *Elevator*, joined Montreal's critically acclaimed Wolf Parade a short time later.

Once the members had whittled the new repertoire down from about 40 songs to a more workable number, they recorded the tracks in Los Angeles with producer Dave Sardy, who's worked with the Red Hot Chili Peppers, Jet, The Dandy Warhols and The Walkmen, among others.

"Dave had an incredible ability to give us free rein and still stay on track," says Bays about the sessions that created the *Elevator* album. "He became like the fifth member of the band."

Not long after the completion of *Elevator*, DeCaro—who enjoyed writing, recording and playing live, but not the touring lifestyle—elected to leave Hot Hot Heat. He was quickly replaced by San Franciscan guitarist and film school graduate Luke Paquin, who was playing around Los Angeles on his own at the time.

"The first time we met with him, we ended up talking for four hours about music and bands we loved," says Bays of the new addition. "Even before we played a note together, it was a perfect fit."

With the success of *Make Up The Breakdown*, Hot Hot Heat left Sub Pop and the indie world behind to sign with Sire Records and WEA International, which released the more mature yet still irrepressibly catchy and danceable *Elevator* in April 2005. The hook-filled first single and video "Goodnight Goodnight" introduced the album, and "Middle Of Nowhere" and "You Owe Me An IOU" followed on both radio stations and video outlets.

The band moved from Victoria to Vancouver, but the guys didn't spend much time there as they went globetrotting almost immediately upon *Elevator*'s launch to give fans a taste of the new songs.

"It has its ups and downs," Hawthorne says of the nomadic lifestyle. "For a good portion of this record I didn't have a loved one at home, so I didn't care. Now that I do, I get homesick frequently."

Luckily, the group has learned how to write songs on the road and can practice them during sound checks. By late 2005, Hot Hot Heat had added three new numbers to its live set, and a couple of others were almost there.

"I'm kind of interested in seeing where this next record's going to go," says Hawthorne. "I certainly learned a lot from recording the last record, and I think that we can do a way better job this time around."

Some of the songs that didn't make the cut for *Elevator* and acoustic versions of some that did have been released as B-sides to singles in the UK. But there are no plans to release the tracks in North America. The tentative strategy was for Hot Hot Heat to start recording a new album in April 2006 in advance of a summer or fall release.

"We obviously have very high hopes for the next record," offers Paquin. "I still feel that we haven't made the record that we're capable of making, so that's what we're going to try to do."

the tragically hip

Gord Sinclair (bass) and Rob Baker (guitar) grew up across the street from each other in Kingston, Ontario. They met Gord Downie (vocals) and Johnny Fay (drums) in high school when they played in several short-lived bands, including one called The Rodents that was referenced years later in the video for "Poets."

When The Tragically Hip (which took its name from a skit in Mike Nesmith's *Elephant Parts*) formed at Queen's University, Paul Langlois (guitar) wasn't yet in the band, but a saxophone player named Davis Manning briefly was. That was back in 1983, and the group has been making music ever since, becoming one of the most popular Canadian bands of all time in the process.

The band's first gig as The Tragically Hip—comprised mainly of songs by the likes of The Rolling Stones, Creedence Clearwater Revival and The Yardbirds—was at the Kingston Artists Association. By the summer of 1986, when Langlois replaced Manning, the group was making four-track demo recordings of original material to send to record companies and playing bars across Ontario up to six nights a week. The band attracted the attention of Jake Gold, who became its manager for almost 20 years as part of the Management Trust, which was co-founded with prominent pollster Allan Gregg.

By this point The Hip (as the group has become known to many fans) had enough original material to go into a studio with Ken Greer (Red Rider) and record a self-titled seven-song EP that was released in Kingston in December 1987 and distributed nationally the next month. The group played about 200 shows from January to September 1988 before it signed a deal with MCA Records, which remastered the EP, added the song "All Canadian Surf Club," and made it available in March 1989.

While the EP wasn't a huge hit, The Hip gained valuable exposure through the singles and videos "Last American Exit" and "Small Town Bringdown." The record continued to sell steadily as the band's fame rose in succeeding years, and by 2005, it had sold 350,000 copies.

The Hip traveled to Memphis, Tennessee, in January 1989 to record its second record, *Up To Here*, at Ardent Studios with producer Don Smith, who had recently worked with Tom Petty, Keith Richards, Roy Orbison and The Traveling Wilburys. With the propulsive hits and everlasting concert favorites "Blow At High Dough," "New Orleans Is Sinking," "Boots Or Hearts" and "38 Years Old," *Up To Here* launched the Hip to stardom.

The album earned the Hip a 1990 Juno Award for most promising group, and the band's thrilling live shows, highlighted by

The Tragically Hip (L to R): Gord Sinclair, Gord Downie, Paul Langlois, Rob Baker, Johnny Fay (2004)

Downie's animated movements, swung the vote in its favor for the Canadian entertainer of the year title at the 1991 Juno show. "I've likened being on stage to being on a hot griddle," Downie said of his stage antics in a February 16, 1995 *SEE Magazine* article. "When the music is pumping, it makes you do strange things. Because I don't play an instrument, I have to do something with my hands and body to allow me to get my words across. I don't spend a lot of time thinking about what I do on stage. It's a performance. It's going wherever the moment takes you and trusting in your body and voice."

Up To Here has gone on to sell 1.25 million copies, making it The Hip's all-time bestseller. It also set the stage for 1991's *Road Apples*, which was produced by Smith in New Orleans, Louisiana. While the album may have had a bit more of a southern rock vibe, "Born In The Water" and "Three Pistols" featured Canadian lyrical references that helped galvanize support in Canada.

The Canadian allusions are something that the Hip has become known for, and some critics cite its Canadian-ness as a primary reason behind the band never becoming as popular internationally as it likely deserves to be. "Over the years, we have written some songs that refer to Canadian events specifically, and others that reflect our response as Canadians to other themes and issues because of who we are and how we've been raised," said Sinclair in a November 5, 1996 canoe.ca article.

"That's where it begins and ends for us. We'd never write a song because it was Canadian, nor would we avoid it. If some of our fans can only identify with us on a nationalistic level, instead of a musical one, then I think that reflects more on them than it does on us."

Road Apples spawned the singles "Little Bones," "Three Pistols," "Long Time Running" and "On The Verge," which helped make The Tragically Hip a household name across Canada. The album has sold more than 900,000 copies domestically.

Fully Completely followed quickly in 1992, the same year the Hip made its first trip to Australia. The album, produced by Chris Tsangarides (Judas Priest, Thin Lizzy, Concrete Blonde) at Battery Studios in London, England, is hailed by many as the band's best. It's also the group's second-best seller—more than a million copies

have found their way into Canadian homes. "Locked In The Trunk Of A Car," "Courage," "At The Hundredth Meridian," "Looking For A Place To Happen" and "Fifty Mission Cap" were among the hits that the Hip unleashed from the album. The band also played them on its first Another Roadside Attraction tour in 1993. The tour helped expose such acts as Midnight Oil, Crash Vegas, Hothouse Flowers, Daniel Lanois, World Party and Pere Ubu to Hip fanatics across Canada.

The Hip returned to Kingsway Studio in New Orleans to record *Day for Night* (1994) with producer Mark Howard. It was a darker album than its predecessors but boasted majestic power in such songs as "Nautical Disaster," "Greasy Jungle," "So Hard Done By" and "Grace, Too." The disc, which has sold almost 800,000 copies, earned the band five 1995 Juno nominations, and it won the awards for both entertainer and group of the year.

The production team of Mark Howard, Mark Vreeken and the Hip reconvened to record *Trouble at the Henhouse* (1996) in San Francisco, New Orleans and the band's own Bathouse studio in Bath, Ontario, a small town just outside Kingston.

"We've always wanted a long, healthy career as a band, and I guess that's always on the back of our minds and, honestly, we also wanted our own place," said Langlois in an article in the October 31, 1996 issue of *Drop-D Magazine*. "Our own studio, somewhere we could leave our gear and jam and record some stuff when we wanted, and we have that now."

Trouble at the Henhouse, which features such favorites as "Gift Shop" and "Ahead By A Century," has sold almost 600,000 copies. It was named both album of the year and rock album of the year, and the Hip also took the best group prize at the 1997 Juno Awards ceremony.

During the tour in support of *Trouble at the Henhouse*, the Hip recorded a November 23, 1996 concert at the Cobo Arena in Detroit, Michigan, that was released the following year on the 14-track *Live Between Us* album, which has gone on to sell almost 400,000 units.

"The road time is absolutely essential for us," Baker said of the Hip live experience in a July 15, 2002 interview on hiponline.com. "There is a cycle that happens from writing a song, going in (the studio) and recording the song and then to consummate the whole thing you have to get out and perform the song live. Then when you are out performing the songs live you are getting new ideas for the new songs. The cycle is just feeding into itself that way."

Steve Berlin, a member of Los
Lobos who got to know the Hip
on the 1997 Another Roadside
Attraction tour, produced 1998's
Phantom Power at the Bathouse
with the band and Vreeken. The
Hip had been working towards
self-production for years, and
since no one knows its music
better, they felt that the time
was finally right.

"Poets," "Something On," "Bobcaygeon" and "Fireworks" were the
highlights of *Phantom Power*, which has sold more than 400,000
copies. The disc was honored as best rock album at the 1999 Juno
Awards, and "Bobcaygeon" won the best single trophy the following year.

Music @ Work, which featured the hits "My Music At Work" and
"Freak Turbulence," sold more than 200,000 copies and won the
2001 Juno for best rock album. The disc was the second and last
produced by the band, Berlin and Vreeken at the Bathouse.

"I think if we were content to just keep reapplying the same for-
mula over and over, we would get tired of this quickly," Baker said
in a July 15, 2002 interview on hiponline.com. "We were friends
before we were a band, and we formed a band to have fun. There
is no point in doing it if you're not going to enjoy it. The first line
in the operating manual for us is 'Don't do it if it's no fun.'"

Producer Hugh Padgham (David Bowie, The Police, XTC) and
engineer Terry Manning (Led Zeppelin, Shakira, Lenny Kravitz)
were enlisted to work on *In Violet Light* (2002) at Manning's
Compass Point Studios in the Bahamas. Padgham achieved his
goal of capturing the Hip's live energy in the studio while simultaneously showcasing Downie's lyrics. "He [Downie] is a writer,
singer, performer and poet, and that makes him pretty unique in
the music business today," Padgham says.

The album sold more than 100,000 copies on the strength of the singles "It's A Good Life If You Don't Weaken," "Silver Jet" and "The Darkest One," which featured a video with the stars of the cult Canadian television comedy, *Trailer Park Boys*. In addition to releasing *In Violet Light* in 2002, the Hip was enshrined in the Canadian Walk of Fame and appeared in the film *Men with Brooms*. The band recorded "Black Day in July" for the 2003 album, *Beautiful: A Tribute to Gordon Lightfoot* in between releasing its own material.

"If the Rolling Stones and R.E.M. were to have sex, the result would be a five-headed baby called The Tragically Hip," says Adam Kasper (Pearl Jam, Foo Fighters, Queens of the Stone Age), the producer of the band's 2004 album, *In Between Evolution*. The record was the group's first since it left the Management Trust to join the roster of Vancouver-based Macklam/Feldman Management, which also handles the careers of Norah Jones, Diana Krall, Leonard Cohen, Joni Mitchell and Elvis Costello among others.

2004

In Between Evolution features some of the shortest, fastest songs that the Hip has ever recorded, and it included the singles "Vaccination Scar," "It Can't Be Nashville Every Night" and "Summer Is Killing Us." The album sold more than 100,000 copies.

"No Threat" and the acoustic "The New Maybe" were the two new songs included on 2005's *Yer Favourites,* a two-record set comprised of 37 songs chosen by fans. The career retrospective was also included in *Hipeponymous,* which featured the two CDs along with a concert DVD and another DVD containing all of the Hip's videos, short films and a 50-minute documentary called *Macroscopic.*

In addition to fronting the Hip, Downie has released two solo albums: *Coke Machine Glow* (2001) and *Battle Of the Nudes* (2003). Baker and former Odds member Craig Northey have a band called Stripper's Union Local 518 that released a self-titled album in 2005. Sinclair, Fay and Langlois contributed to the record. Langlois launched the Ching Music record label that same year. Its first release was the Hugh Dillon Redemption Choir's *The High Co$t of Low Living,* which Langlois produced.

The Hip had been nominated for 34 Junos and won 11 of them through 2005. That was more than enough to get the band inducted into the Canadian Music Hall of Fame at the 2005 Juno Awards show in Winnipeg.

Later that year the group started working on its next album with Canadian producer Bob Rock, whose previous credits include Aerosmith, Bon Jovi, Metallica, Bryan Adams and Our Lady Peace.

"I still feel like the music I love defines who I am," says Baker. "Making music is what I always wanted to do with my life. I wouldn't know who I was if I wasn't doing this."

"Our main success is that we're still doing it with the same five people after all this time," adds Langlois. "We like to be together, whether it's recording music, having a group meeting, watching a game, or going on the road."

simple plan

Simple Plan wasn't an overnight success, even if that's the impression that most people had after the Montreal band's debut album sold a few million copies around the world.

The group members had been high school friends, and drummer Chuck Comeau, singer Pierre Bouvier and bassist David Desrosiers had played together as teenagers in a punk band called Reset. The group had a relatively small but loyal following after releasing two independent albums in the late '90s on the Union 2112 label.

Two years after Reset's final album hit store shelves, Comeau formed a new band with guitarists Jeff Stinco and Sebastien Lefebvre. After Comeau ran into Bouvier again at a Sugar Ray concert, he asked him to join his fledgling group, which was named after the 1998 film, *A Simple Plan*.

"When we all used to get together in Chuck's basement, which is where we used to rehearse, we were talking about what we wanted to do with this band," says Stinco. "We all decided to quit school and make Simple Plan our main focus. The desire was always to tour and perform, and records were just an excuse to get back on the road and tour. That was the lifestyle that we dreamed about."

The first song that the quartet wrote together was "I'd Do Anything," which later became a hit single. Desrosiers joined the lineup about 10 months later, and the version of Simple Plan that everyone now knows was born.

Early on, Comeau handled most things at the business end, and he became focused on finding Simple Plan a record deal that could make their albums available internationally.

"The hardest thing about Reset was that we got letters from Brazil, from Australia, from California—from people who couldn't find our records or see us live," Comeau said in an interview in the February 2004 issue of *Alternative Press*. "We felt so powerless—how do we put out a record in Australia?"

Comeau found out from his friend Pat Langlois that Lava Records A&R vice-president Andy Karp would be coming to

Simple Plan (L to R): Chuck Comeau, Jeff Stinco, Pierre Bouvier, Sebastien Lefebvre, David Desrosiers (2004)

Montreal to see Rubberman, a band signed to Aquarius Records, the label Langlois worked for. Comeau pulled out all the stops to get the American executive to see his band when he was in town and booked a small venue called Club Zone. The friends sent an invitation to Karp, and the band played under the name Touchdown to protect Langlois from getting in trouble with his employer.

The not-so-simple plan worked. Karp came, liked what he saw and put the wheels in motion to sign the band. Langlois has since become Simple Plan's webmaster and works with the group in a variety of other areas.

After signing with Lava/Warner, Simple Plan released its *No Pads, No Helmets...Just Balls* debut album in 2002. The record was produced by Canadian veteran Arnold Lanni (brother of band manager Rob Lanni), who had previously been at the studio controls for Our Lady Peace's biggest sellers. The album also featured a couple of impressive guests, as Mark Hoppus (Blink-182) sang backing vocals on "I'd Do Anything" and Joel Madden (Good Charlotte) did the same on "You Don't Mean Anything."

Simple Plan's influences range from such timeless pop-rock acts as The Beatles, the Beach Boys and Elvis Costello to punk pioneers The Ramones and The Clash, with more recent favorites like Green Day and Blink-182 thrown in for good measure. These reference points were obvious on *No Pads*, an album full of catchy pop-punk songs of young angst dealing with topics such as love and longing, working dead-end jobs, being alone, infatuation, frustration and parental strife.

Although the band members grew up listening to artists who sang about injustice and world affairs, and Reset often went down that same path, they decided that they wanted to write personal songs about dealing with everyday situations that people could relate to for Simple Plan. "Dealing with seeing your friends of family die, coping with having people and parents look down on what you want to do with your life, being stuck in a town you hate, working a job you can't stand—these are the kind of things we had to go through, and writing about it helped us out," said Comeau in a February 2004 *Alternative Press* article.

While *No Pads* got off to a relatively slow start at retail, the momentum didn't stop once things got rolling. Radio and video play was extensive for the album's four singles: "I'm Just a Kid," "I'd Do Anything," "Addicted" and "Perfect." While the album was certified double platinum in Canada and the U.S., it also went platinum in Australia and gold in Indonesia, Malaysia, Japan, Mexico, New Zealand, the Philippines and Singapore.

Simple Plan toured endlessly, playing with everyone from Aerosmith to Rancid, and was nominated for a handful of honors including a Juno Award and four MTV Video Music Awards. The band won the 2003 MuchMusic Video Award for favorite Canadian group.

2004

The group released a DVD titled *A Big Package For You*, directed by Comeau and produced by Langlois, that included video clips, interviews, backstage footage and a previously unreleased song called "Crash and Burn." It was nominated for a 2004 Juno.

But even after reaching such lofty heights and playing in front of more people with each successive tour, the band members still make a point of meeting fans and signing autographs after every show.

"We don't care if you're 12, 24 or 44, or what color hair you have—if you like our music, you're welcome to come to any of our shows, and we'll be stoked to hang out with you," Bouvier told *Alternative Press* in a February 2004 article.

2005

BaNd tRiViA

Pierre Bouvier hosted the MTV reality series *Damage Control*, where parents pretended they were going away for the weekend but then spied on what their teenagers did in their absence on cameras hidden around the house.

Since many of Simple Plan's young fans relate so well to the band's music and messages, they appreciate their heroes being so accessible and are thrilled to get a chance to meet and speak with them. And the group members often get as much out of the meetings as the fans.

"We meet tons of kids at the shows and get tons of emails and letters from people who tell us about how our songs helped them out," said Bouvier in a February 2004 *Alternative Press* article. "We heard so many sad stories that choked us up big time. A girl got the lyrics to 'Meet You There' tattooed on her arm after her best friend killed herself.

"A girl who never got along with her dad and hadn't talked to him in seven years played him "Perfect" as he was in a hospital bed dying of cancer. They spent the last week of his life trying to catch up with each other."

When it came time for a second album, Comeau and Bouvier spent three months writing new songs in Vancouver. "I think on the first record we just wanted to write a pure pop-punk record, and on this one we didn't care— we just wanted to write good songs," says Comeau.

The band enlisted Bob Rock (the man behind some of the biggest records from Metallica, Mötley Crüe and Bon Jovi) to produce the album *Still Not Getting Any...*, which was released in 2004. While the disc followed a similar musical path as its predecessor, it was also heavier in certain places and featured a string section on "One" and "Untitled." The album spawned four singles and videos ("Welcome to My Life," "Shut Up!" "Untitled" and "Crazy") and racked up more impressive sales certifications: triple platinum in Canada; double platinum in Australia and Indonesia; platinum in Malaysia, New Zealand, Singapore and the U.S.; and gold in Japan, Mexico, Thailand and the Philippines.

Simple Plan was nominated for a group of the year Juno, while *Still Not Getting Any...* was a finalist for best album and best pop album. The group traveled around the globe in support of *Still Not Getting Any...* before returning home to do its first major coast-to-coast Canadian tour in November 2005 in support of its *MTV Hard Rock Live* enhanced CD.

"We had released a pretty simple live recording in Japan, and some people heard about it and wanted us to do the same thing in North America," Stinco explains about the MTV release, which also features a bonus acoustic version of "Crazy." The Orlando, Florida show where the album was recorded was also taped for an MTV special.

Along with television and video exposure, which has certainly given a huge boost to Simple Plan's career, the band has also contributed to a number of films. The group submitted the previously unreleased "Grow Up" for the first *Scooby-Doo* film soundtrack in 2002 because all of the band members were fans of the Saturday morning cartoon. They were then asked to write the lead track ("I Don't Wanna Think About You") for the 2004 sequel, *Scooby-Doo 2: Monsters Unleashed*.

Simple Plan also covered The Turtles' "Happy Together" for the *Freaky Friday* soundtrack, covered Cheap Trick's "Surrender" for the *Fantastic Four* soundtrack, contributed an acoustic version of "Perfect" to *Confessions of a Teenage Drama Queen*, and had "I'm Just A Kid" used in *The New Guy*.

The group made its big screen debut in 2004's *New York Minute*, playing the band that Mary-Kate Olsen's character, Roxanne Ryan, idolizes. "Vacation" appeared on the soundtrack.

While kids and consumers have certainly embraced Simple Plan, many critics haven't been as friendly and have occasionally

labeled the group as a pre-packaged boy band. But Comeau insists that such assertions are totally off base, as the group members are involved with the look of the CD packages, contribute to video treatments and have input into photo shoots and who they tour with. Comeau, Bouvier and Langlois also have a clothing company called Role Model that designs the band's merchandise.

After completing a major European tour early in 2006, the band members planned to start working on a new album, which was expected to be released before the end of the year.

> "We're going to take whatever time it takes to get some songs together," says Stinco. "We don't really write a lot on the road. The schedule is pretty hectic and there are a lot of distractions. The same thing happened for *Still Not Getting Any*.

"We hadn't written a lot of material on tour because it's not something that we're very comfortable doing. But we had an idea of where we wanted to go. And with this record, we've also been discussing a lot about direction and what we want to do. I think it's going to be different. You stop being artistic when you release the same record over and over. For us, it's really important to change things up and try new things."

arcade fire

Arcade Fire is one of the most exciting, and least likely, success stories to emerge from the Canadian music scene over the past few years.

The group was formed by Texan Win Butler, the grandson of swing-era bandleader Alvino Rey, who followed a friend to Montreal to study music and religion at McGill University. He met Régine Chassagne, the francophone daughter of Haitian parents who fled the island's repressive regime in the '60s. Chassagne often performed in a medieval music ensemble or sang jazz standards while studying music. The two bonded on many levels. Chassagne joined one of the early incarnations of Arcade Fire, and the pair eventually married in August 2003.

Butler, Chassagne and the other members of Arcade Fire spent part of the summer of 2002 at Butler's parents' property in Maine, creating a makeshift studio and recording a seven-song EP. Tension was in the air, and members Dane Mills and Brendan Reed left the eclectic group shortly after the band self-released the limited-edition *Arcade Fire* EP in early 2003. More than once, it looked like the band wouldn't survive. But a new and more passionate lineup was formed, and the Arcade Fire excitement started to spread.

The group's name is based on a tall tale that was told to Butler when he was a child about a fire that burned down an arcade and killed all the kids inside. Though the story wasn't true, the young Butler had believed it, and the words "arcade fire" stayed with him to adulthood. The name seems appropriate, too, considering how the band can be both playful (group members often don helmets so that others in the band can use them as human percussion instruments) and intense in its performances.

The Arcade Fire that recorded the debut album included Butler (guitar, lead vocals, bass, keyboards, harmonica), Chassagne (keyboards, lead and backing vocals, accordion, xylophone, drums), Richard Parry (guitar, percussion, helmet, backing vocals, upright bass, keyboards), Tim Kingsbury (bass, backing vocals, guitar), Win's younger brother Will Butler (percussion, helmet, guitar, bass, backing vocals) and Howard Bilerman (drums). Other guests—

The Arcade Fire (L to R): Win Butler, Régine Chassagne, Tim Kingsbury, Richard Parry (2004)

BaNd tRiViA

including violinists Sarah Neufeld, who's now a full-time member, and Owen Pallett, who later joined the touring version of Arcade Fire—contributed violin, cello, horns, harp, viola and drums.

Bilerman is also an audio engineer who co-runs Montreal's Hotel 2 Tango studio—a magnet for the city's coolest independent bands. He saw something special in Butler and the rest of the group after recording two songs with them. "It's refreshing to see a band—and I'm talking about all of them—who care more about making music than being successful at making music, and who work on music and live up to the responsibility that I think should be involved in putting out a record," he said in a September 2004 article in *Exclaim!*

In between recording sessions in August 2003 and the winter of the following year, Arcade Fire honed its reputation as one of the most exciting live acts around. During their performances, members swapped instruments and used their stage surroundings, and each other, as tools for creating percussion. It wasn't unusual to see the group leave the stage and weave their way through the audience, chanting and playing. All of this happened with an intensity that would leave the musicians exhausted, if not sick, after most performances.

"The live show is very much an experiment," said Win Butler in a February 14, 2005 pitchforkmedia.com interview. "We always try different things live, and I feel this certain kind of energy is really natural to these songs. I don't know that we'll always be puking our guts out for a whole show. It's definitely draining. But it's the type of thing we're interested in right now."

Arcade Fire isn't interested in simply recreating the music from its album on stage. Things often go in different directions as the various members get into their own grooves, and the playing and singing becomes more aggressive. The music threatens to spiral out of control, which adds a sense of excitement for the audience, but very rarely actually gets away from the musicians.

Parry described an Arcade Fire concert in a January 10, 2005 interview on heraclitussayz.com.

"Our live show is a bit of a different beast than the album, and we aren't trying to be all that faithful to keeping the music sounding exactly like the album—more trying to just do something special live. A lot of people seem to like the live show better. It's sorta like a more punk rock version of the record. Whatever that means."

Talk began circulating about the live performances, and the songs from the EP made it on to the Internet in MP3 format, where file-sharing spread them much farther than the limited sales of the physical CD ever could. Perhaps more than any band of the last few years, Arcade Fire benefited hugely from grassroots word-of-mouth support that spread across blogs and music publications to create a cult-like following months before the debut album was even released.

"Everyone in this band has been profoundly inspired by a musical moment or another, enough that they have to make something special happen themselves," said Parry in the September 2004 issue of *Exclaim!* "That's the nature of any quasi-spiritual or inspirational moment. It doesn't really let go of you. You have to put some of that back into the world."

This buzz got several independent record companies from Canada and the U.S. interested in Arcade Fire. But after much discussion, the group elected in May 2004 to sign a two-album deal with Merge Records—a small label based in Chapel Hill, North Carolina, run by Superchunk frontman Mac McCaughan, that's also home to such respected indie-rock acts as Destroyer, Spoon, The Magnetic Fields and The Essex Green. The band members thought their music would fit well at Merge and liked the people who worked for the label.

> "It was really important to me to have the people who are putting out our record be in bands themselves—to feel a certain kinship with them, but also to know they've been down the same road," explained Bilerman in a June 17, 2004 article in *NOW* magazine.

To satisfy the diehards, in the summer of 2004, Merge released 1500 copies of a seven-inch vinyl single featuring "Neighborhood No. 1 (Tunnels)" and, on the B-side, a 1940s broadcast of "My Buddy"—a song recorded by Butler's grandfather that was the last song played at his funeral.

Funerals had been such a common occurrence for Arcade Fire members in the time leading up to the release of their debut album that they titled it *Funeral*. Chassagne's grandmother, Butler's grandfather and Parry's aunt died between June 2003 and April 2004. Butler insists, however, that *Funeral* wasn't designed as a concept album based around death, despite what critics may believe. He says the band members didn't realize how much influence the deaths had until after the record was finished. "When we started listening to the album afterward, though, it was clear that this played a part in what we were doing," he said in a January 16, 2005 *LA Times* article.

Funeral was recorded for less than $10,000 in the hope that the group could get its investment back so that they could make a second album. It was released in North America in September 2004. A rave review on the influential pitchforkmedia.com website and a dynamic showcase at the CMJ Music Festival in New York City got even more tongues wagging, and Arcade Fire suddenly found itself hailed as the next big thing by the musical cognoscenti. *Funeral*—which blissfully combines indie-rock, chamber pop, new wave and choral influences with lyrics sung in both English and French—made several critics' year-end top 10 lists.

The band didn't want Merge to do any intensive marketing for the release. In the April–May 2005 issue of *Magnet*, Butler said, "Ashlee Simpson's record sells a million copies in a week, and not because it's an awesome record. They sold it really well because they marketed it, and I think that approach has negative

implications on the culture. For us, ideally, if someone buys our record, they've heard about us from a couple of different places. If my friend tells me something's good, then maybe I hear a song, then I read something about it, then I'm actually getting information about something—not just responding to an ad—and can then find out if I like it."

Funeral also earned Arcade Fire such prominent fans as David Byrne, who joined the band on stage to perform the Talking Heads' "This Must Be the Place (Naïve Melody)," which was later released as the B-side of a UK single, and David Bowie, who gushed about the band in the March 10, 2005 issue of *Rolling Stone.* "There's a certain uninhibited passion in the Arcade Fire's huge, dense recording sound. They meld everything from early Motown, French *chanson* and Talking Heads through to the Cure in a kaleidoscopic dizzy sort of rush."

Merge initially pressed 10,000 copies of *Funeral,* but demand grew so quickly that the company couldn't keep up. The problem was made worse by the Juno Award-nominated cardboard packaging (which included a sepia-toned insert modeled after Rey's wake program) that took longer to produce than a normal plastic CD jewel case. The short supply fueled the fire, and it wasn't long before *Funeral* surpassed Neutral Milk Hotel's *The Aeroplane Over the Sea* as Merge's biggest seller ever.

While momentum continued to grow in North America as Arcade Fire toured, *Funeral* was released in Australia and the UK in February 2005 and in Japan in July of that year. Butler had been confident that the band members' hard work would get people interested and out to their shows, but the speed of the group's increasing popularity was beyond anything he had imagined.

Bilerman returned to his studio duties, and drummer and guitarist Jeremy Gara took his place on the road. The band had originally booked small clubs, but overwhelming interest forced moves to larger venues as it played throughout Canada, the U.S., Europe and at the SummerSonic Festival in Japan. In addition to its Juno nomination for the album cover artwork, *Funeral* was also one of the finalists in the best alternative album category.

"I don't think this band is super-focused on being innovative for innovation's sake," Butler said in an October 2004 article posted on tinymixtapes.com. "Our sound comes from us playing together, and our songs that we write are about things we care about, and when we're making a record we try to add stuff until it doesn't make us sick to hear it and we're happy with the way it sounds. You don't choose your influences; I know I haven't chosen my influences. It doesn't really work that way in the creation process."

The band took a break from touring in April 2005 and returned to Montreal to record the "Cold Wind" single with producer Chris Thomas, who previously worked with Roxy Music, Pink Floyd, Brian Eno and the Sex Pistols. The song was used in the HBO television series *Six Feet Under* and earned the band a Grammy Award nomination for best song written for a motion picture, television or other visual media. *Funeral* also received a Grammy nod for best alternative music album.

The underground buzz on Arcade Fire grew to the point where it was featured on the April 4, 2005 cover of the Canadian edition of *Time* magazine, which hailed the band by saying it "helped put Canadian music on the world map."

The group signed a deal with EMI Music Publishing the next month, which helped land the band's normal show-opener, "Wake Up," on UK commercials for the BBC's fall TV season. The majestic "Wake Up" was also used as the recorded introductory song for U2 on its 2005 world tour, and the Irish group invited Arcade Fire to open some of its shows and join them onstage.

Bowie joined Arcade Fire onstage to perform "Wake Up" on the *Fashion Rocks* TV special, and he also collaborated with the group on versions of his classic hits "Life on Mars" and "Five Years," which were only available for a limited time as digital downloads on iTunes.

People who had been spending exorbitant amounts on the original EP on eBay, or who were forced to buy bootleg copies, caught a break when Merge (and Rough Trade in the UK) gave in

2004

to consumer demand and released a remastered version of the disc in the summer.

With all of the attention being heaped upon Arcade Fire, radio and TV outlets finally took notice. The hypnotically catchy "Rebellion (Lies)" single and video received wide exposure and helped push sales of *Funeral* past the platinum mark in Canada and gold in the UK. As of November 2005, the album had sold more than 500,000 copies around the world—an almost unheard of figure for a band on such a small label.

> Major record companies tried to muscle in and get a piece of the action, but Arcade Fire was adamant that it would stick with Merge for its second album despite the bigger budget that a larger company could offer them.

The group earned enough money, however, to purchase an old church outside of Montreal that it planned on converting into a studio to record the next album. The group also wants to assemble material for a future DVD release. "We're all super-excited to cut ourselves off from the outside world and get recording," Butler said in a July 18, 2005 MTV.com article.

With all the success that has come Arcade Fire's way in the last two years, some people might expect the band to rest on its laurels. But Chassagne insists that there's no chance of that happening. "I'm never content," she said in the September 2004 issue of *Exclaim!*

"For me, I'm always at zero trying to get to square one. For me, I haven't achieved anything yet. This is a start."

default

While changing the name of your band to a default choice can potentially confuse your fans, the members of this Vancouver quartet didn't experience any fallout when they made a switch in 2000.

The Fallout was formed in 1999 by guitarist Jeremy Hora and drummer Danny Craig, who'd been playing music around the city for four years. But since neither of them were singers, they needed one. They discovered that a longtime friend, who had never sung outside of his car or his shower, was interested. Dallas Smith (named by his hockey-loving father after Bobby Orr's defence partner on the '70s Boston Bruins) auditioned—and nailed it.

It wasn't too long before they started laying down some tracks with engineer Joey Moi, who passed along a tape to friend and Nickelback frontman Chad Kroeger. He called the band right away and said that he wanted to work with them. Kroeger even helped Smith convince his father to lend the band $20,000 from his retirement fund to allow them to record. The band spent the fall of '99 in the studio with Kroeger and playing local shows to give Smith a feel for what it's like to play in front of people.

"I feel that the fact that Jeremy, Danny and myself were friends when Default was formed gave us a big advantage," Smith said in a 2001 interview with smother.net. "We were not afraid to bring ideas to the band, and we were also not afraid to tell each other that some ideas sucked."

They entered local radio station CFOX's homegrown talent competition and beat out more than 300 other acts to land one of four spots on the *Vancouver Seeds* compilation. When the guys realized that there were several other acts called the Fallout around North America, they hatched the name Default.

CFOX received great listener feedback from the song "Deny," which drove sales of the *Seeds* CD and boosted local interest in Default's independently released album, *The Fallout*. When sales of the disc exceeded 2000 in short order, record companies started paying attention. Canadian and American labels tabled offers, but the band opted to go with New York-based TVT Records because it didn't ask Default to change its approach and go for a slightly heavier sound.

Default kept eight of the tracks produced by Kroeger (who also co-wrote six of the songs) from the indie album for the TVT debut. Then, with new bassist Dave Benedict (who had worked

Default (L to R): Danny Craig, Jeremy Hora, Dallas Smith, Dave Benedict (2005)

with Hora at a car dealership) in tow, the group went south to Seattle to record with producer Rick Parashar, whose intimidating resumé included albums by Pearl Jam, Candlebox, Alice In Chains and other leading lights of the grunge rock movement, which was born in his hometown.

Default spent more than two weeks at Parashar's London Bridge Studios, where they came away unscathed after an earthquake that severely damaged some buildings in Seattle's downtown core. The group also came away with three more songs—"Wasting My Time," "Sick and Tired" and "Live a Lie"—which gave it 11 for the completely remastered version of *The Fallout* that was released by TVT on July 17, 2001.

"We know as a band we're right down the middle of the line," Smith said in the December 2003 issue of *Chart*. "We're not breaking any barriers, we're not trying to reinvent anything, we're just kind of playing old fashioned rock 'n' roll."

Straight-ahead, riff-driven rock was just what fans, and radio and video programmers, seemed to be looking for. The album spawned four singles: "Deny," "Live a Lie," "Sick and Tired" and, most importantly, "Wasting My Time." That melodic but crunching

2005

power ballad became one of the biggest rock hits of the year in both Canada and the U.S. Fans were able to put a face to the band when Nickelback took Default on tour as its supporting act. The tour helped raise Default's profile; it also fully introduced the group to the debauchery of the rock lifestyle.

"When Nickelback first took us out, we were wild," Smith said in the December 2003 issue of *Chart*. "Chad every night would say, 'Party's on the blue bus,' which was ours, and he'd actually ride on our bus to the next town, and we'd just be drinking until, like, five in the morning. It was unbelievably crazy. It was a lot of fun, but hopefully it never gets that wild again."

Default stayed on the road in support of the album, opening for other bands and headlining its own shows. All the while, the group was performing on late-night television shows and getting valuable radio and video exposure. Most notable on the video front was the clip for "Deny" that featured the band members being pummeled in a boxing ring by female champion Laila Ali, daughter of Muhammad Ali. The video hit number one on MuchMusic, and the group received four MuchMusic Video Award nominations in 2002.

And though Default didn't appear in *Spider-Man*, it got a major shot in the arm by landing the previously unreleased song "Blind" on the soundtrack to one of the biggest blockbuster movies of 2002. A previously unreleased acoustic version of "Deny" was placed on the *Swimfan* soundtrack that same year.

The Fallout went on to sell more than a million copies in the U.S. and more than 100,000 in Canada. A limited edition CD/DVD version of the album—featuring "Blind" and acoustic versions of "Wasting My Time" and "Deny," as well as music videos, a concert video and MTV's 25-minute Default *Rockumentary*—was released in November 2002.

If that wasn't enough, Default again followed in Nickelback's footsteps and captured the 2002 Juno Award for best new group.

Default took the "Don't fix it if it ain't broke" approach when it came time to make its next album and worked with a lot of the same people from the first time around. The band wrote six songs on its own and also co-wrote with Kroeger, Parashar, Jim Vallance (a frequent Bryan Adams collaborator) and Butch Walker (Marvelous 3). Parashar produced nine tracks, Walker worked on two, and Kroeger and Moi were responsible for one. The sound and the lyrical content also stayed on the same path, sticking with the relationship-based themes of the previous release.

Elocation was released in November 2003, and the band once again hit the road to support the new record. The group toured on its own and supported Evanescence while releasing three singles: "Throw It All Away," "(Taking My) Life Away" and "All She Wrote".

Elocation also included a cover of Jeff Buckley's "Cruel," which featured Gordie Johnson (Big Sugar) playing slide guitar. "We were looking for a song to cover, like a really obscure B-side that nobody's ever heard of, and our A&R guy at the label gave me the *Songs to No One* CD," says Smith of the choice.

"That song really jumped out at me. We put our own spin on it and put some balls to it, and that was it."

For whatever reason, the songs on *Elocation* didn't catch on as much as those from *The Fallout*—especially in the U.S. While the album was certified gold in Canada, south of the border it only sold about 10 percent of its predecessor. While Smith doesn't think that TVT did as good a job in promoting and marketing *Elocation* as it did with *The Fallout*, he conceded that the band might have been too complacent in working toward the second album. Still, *Elocation* was nominated for a 2005 Juno for best rock album.

2005

Some critics might place part of the blame for the drop in popularity on Default sounding too much like Nickelback and other "nu grunge" guitar rock bands like Creed, Staind and Theory Of A Deadman. "I can see why there is a comparison," Smith admits. "I'm not insulted by it. They're great bands, and they sell records and have success. It's better than being compared to a sh**ty band."

But Default knew that the pressure was on for its crucial third album, and it wanted to carve out a more distinct niche for itself by adding more layering and counter-melodies to the music, showcasing Smith's vocal range, reducing the focus on relationships in its lyrics and bringing in new collaborators. The group members decided to draw on their last few years on the road for inspiration and spent a year writing songs on their own and with producer

Bob Marlette and songwriter-for-hire Marti Frederickson (who's penned hits for Aerosmith, Sheryl Crow, Faith Hill and Pink).

"Bob's worked with everyone from Tracy Chapman to Black Sabbath to a bunch of jazz groups," Smith says of the band's choice of Marlette to produce the album. "We may not be trying to be a metal band, but the way Bob works, even our ballads have balls now."

One Thing Remains was released in October 2005. Its first single and video, "Count On Me," was produced by Moi and Kroeger (who also co-wrote the song). The Nickelback leader has remained a constant friend and a source of both ideas and inspiration to Default, according to Smith. The fact that both bands share the same manager, Union Entertainment Group's Bryan Coleman, also keeps them in close contact.

Default went back on the road with Nickelback in the U.S. in early 2006 before returning home for an extensive coast-to-coast Canadian tour. "I've never really noticed any differences between fans in the U.S. and Canada," says Smith.

"We prefer to play in Canada to Canadian crowds, which are usually better, but a good crowd's a good crowd. It always depends on how many times a week we're being played on a radio station in the town we're in. That's pretty much what it comes down to."

While German and Australian releases were secured for *One Thing Remains*, Default decided to concentrate its energy on North America before promoting the album overseas.

"We're not really paying attention to what's going on past there because we know we need a story here to have any success anywhere else," says Smith. "First things first."

the new pornographers

If the members of The New Pornographers were a little more famous, you could probably get away with calling the ensemble a supergroup. But they should be quite content in the knowledge that a growing number of people consider them to be a super group.

The band was put together in Vancouver by former Zumpano singer, songwriter and guitarist Carl Newman in 1997 as a studio project for him and his friends. The group included singer and songwriter Dan Bejar (Destroyer), alternative country chanteuse Neko Case, drummer Kurt Dahle (Limblifter), guitarist and keyboard player Todd Fancey (Limblifter), bassist John Collins (The Evaporators) and filmmaker Blaine Thurier (who figured out how to play keyboards once he was invited to join in the fun).

"I want us to be a party band," said Newman in an article in the June 11, 2003 issue of *Seattle Weekly*. "That's all I've ever tried to do."

They easily succeeded in becoming that, and they came up with an amusing name to match their fun-loving attitude. Newman stresses that the moniker was adopted before he learned that disgraced televangelist Jimmy Swaggart had written a book titled *Music: The New Pornography*.

The group first gained attention when its "Letter From An Occupant," a soaring piece of pop sung by Case, appeared on the 2000 Mint Records benefit compilation, *The Good Jacket Presents... Vancouver Special*. The song was also one of the highlights of The New Pornographers' *Mass Romantic* debut album, which came out later that year on Mint, a small trend-setting Vancouver label that has released records from performers including Case, Carolyn Mark, The Smugglers, Duotang and Huevos Rancheros.

Newman and Bejar wrote all the songs on the record, which was brimming with power-pop-influenced indie rock that sounded fresh and original even when it borrowed influences from the past.

"There aren't that many egos in the band because everybody has their own different thing that they do," says Newman. "It's not like Neko is going, 'I want to get one of my songs into the New Pornographers.' What does she care? She has her own solo projects. Dan's at the other end of it. You have to bug Dan to get songs. It's not like his songs are getting cut or anything. Everyone that wants to write songs has a vehicle to do it, so the Pornographers are generally left to me for the most part."

2005

Despite the record's diverse instrumentation, often complex arrangements and different vocalists, *Mass Romantic* was a surprisingly cohesive album. And to the surprise of many, it went on to sell 65,000 copies, making numerous critics' year-end top-10 lists and capturing the 2001 Juno Award for best alternative album.

The band members were surprised by the disc's success. They expected *Mass Romantic* to have limited appeal, and there were no plans in place for a second album. Just finishing the first seemed like a triumph.

In 2002, Mint signed an international licensing deal for The New Pornographers with Matador Records, the hip New York–based label that has put out records from such diverse and respected acts as Yo La Tengo, Sleater-Kinney, Guided By Voices, The Soft Boys and The Fall. Matador has a network of European distributors that opened up a new continent for The New Pornographers to exploit.

FUBAR, a Canadian comedy about two heavy metal-loving hosers, developed a cult following when it hit theatres in 2002. A big part of its attraction was its soundtrack that featured several Canuck bands covering rock hits of the '70s. The New Pornographers' contribution, a version of Toronto's "Your Daddy Don't Know," was one of the best songs on the compilation. But Newman says that the band has too many of its own songs to concern itself with recording any more covers.

Bejar declined to play live with The New Pornographers, which had to limit its performances anyway because the members were so busy with their other projects. But this gave Newman and Bejar more time to come up with songs for the group's sophomore effort, 2003's *Electric Version*. Although it was a bit more refined than *Mass Romantic*, it was still overflowing with infectiously catchy power-pop and rock songs.

Thurier directed the videos for the disc's two singles, "The Laws Have Changed" and "All for Swinging You Around," both of which were sung by Case—who was named the "Sexiest Babe of Indie Rock" in a Playboy.com poll.

"We have big drumbeats and a good female singer," Newman said in the June 11, 2003 issue of *Seattle Weekly*. "It was always my theory that if you had those elements, you'd become popular. When I write a song that sounds like a hit, I say, let's get Neko to sing this one."

Like *Mass Romantic*, *Electric Version* became one of the most critically acclaimed albums of the year. Even better, it moved 20,000 more copies than the debut and became Mint's biggest seller ever.

All of this was accomplished with songs featuring lyrics that weren't exactly easy to decipher. But Newman compares his words to the poems of e.e. cummings—they may not make a lot of sense upon first reading, but offer more insight the more you study them. He isn't too preoccupied with whether people figure out what he's trying to convey. "I'm always a lot more concerned with the sound of the words. That comes first, and then I bend it. I have the melody and the sound of words, and then I try to bend that into some kind of narrative. That's the tough part."

With Case's solo career still going strong and the group hoping to do more touring in support of the next album, Newman looked for another female voice to add to the New Pornographers' mix. He just didn't expect that it would be a niece that he didn't even know he had when he began his music career: Kathryn Calder, who sings and plays keyboards in Victoria, BC group Immaculate Machine.

The New Pornographers (L to R): (back row) Todd Fancey, John Collins, Blaine Thurier; (front row) Carl Newman, Kurt Dahle, Neko Case (2005)

"About seven years ago I found out I had a long-lost sister, who had two kids," Newman says. "I knew Kathryn became a musician, but only recently friends saw her band play and raved to me about her talent. I thought, 'You can't have your niece in your band. It's just not done.' It turns out that it is done."

And although Newman gave Case the most immediately appealing, potentially radio-friendly songs to sing on the previous albums, he took a different approach this time. "In the past she'd been given the pop hits, and this time I wanted to give her the slower songs. I thought it would be good to screw around with them and give her the ballads, because it's not what people would expect," is how he explained the assignment of vocal parts in an article in the September 2005 issue of *Chart*.

Since Case spent a grand total of about eight days recording her parts for the three albums, the group's other members deserved some time in the spotlight, too, despite how much fans loved the singer's incredible voice. Unlike Case, with her busy solo career, The New Pornographers is the other members' main project, and they spend much more time coming up with the group's songs and recording them.

The group's third album, *Twin Cinema*, isn't as frantic as *Mass Romantic* or as eclectic as *Electric Version*. With its slightly slower tempo, it doesn't have the immediate impact of the first two records. "Sometimes you can overload and put too much stuff in a song, and we've been guilty of doing that," admits Newman.

But the listener discovers more of *Twin Cinema*'s subtle charms with each play. "We consciously wanted to change it up a little," says Newman.

"Retain what made the first two albums great, but move in new directions. I wanted it to be more sweeping and sprawling, to have the songs move dynamically, both internally and from song to song. We wanted to see if we could make a record that isn't referred to as 'the windows down, car-stereo-blasting summer album of the year,' if only once."

> *Twin Cinema* was released in August 2005 and debuted at number 40 on the Canadian sales chart and at number 44 on the *Billboard* chart in the U.S. It sold more than 5000 units in the first month at home and another 43,000 during that time south of the border and looks likely to eclipse *Electric Version* as Mint's biggest seller.

The video for *Twin Cinema*'s first single, "Use It," was directed by Thurier and included cameos by American comic and actor David Cross and Vancouver gonzo journalist Nardwuar the Human Serviette. American Michael Palmieri, who has previously shot clips for the Foo Fighters and Beck, directed the video for the second single, "Sing Me Spanish Techno." "He was willing to do it cheap because he's a fan," says Newman.

While The New Pornographers was forced to use four different lineups to accommodate members' schedules, the group toured more than ever before in support of *Twin Cinema*. Even Bejar took part in some shows. The band played across North America and also did a couple of short European tours encompassing the UK, Germany and Austria in the fall of 2005, and it embarked on another North American tour in early 2006. Newman says that audience sizes have been increasing with each successive trip.

"There's something nice about pulling into a town and having hundreds or thousands of people waiting to see you. I think that makes it a lot easier. It's still draining sometimes, but it can be much more draining when you're showing up and playing for hardly anybody. It makes you not want to do it at all."

Although Newman admits that writing new material on the road isn't easy, he was doing it in hope of being able to record a new album in the first half of 2006. In a November 10, 2005 MTV.com article, he explains that he has so many half-written songs that writing for a new album doesn't mean starting from scratch. "Whenever I'm going through a mental block, I'll just sort through old demos I've recorded and go, 'Yeah, this is good.'"

2005

While The New Pornographers' career has paralleled the explosion of independent Canadian bands that have burst on to the international scene this decade, the group members have done things the way they want and have made music that's easily identifiable as their own. Newman believes that this will help the band have a lengthier career than many of its contemporaries.

"I think what we've got going for us is that we don't have anything to do with any specific scene. I think that there are bands that are part of this indie revival that's been huge in the past couple of years that aren't going to have longevity because people will always go, 'Oh, they were part of that fad.' People aren't going to want to listen to them in a few years because it's going to be the equivalent of wearing bell-bottoms."

Whatever pants the members of The New Pornographers choose to wear, they can be assured of a loyal following as long as they keep making music as vital, interesting and just plain fun as what they've given us to this point.

the trews

If you're going to play 400 shows in two years, you'd better be a pretty close-knit group. And the four members of The Trews are definitely that.

Brothers Colin (vocals, guitar) and John-Angus MacDonald (guitar, vocals), St. John's, Newfoundland-born cousin Sean Dalton (drum, vocals) and longtime friend Jack Syperek (bass, vocals) formed a band called Trouser in 2001 in their hometown of Antigonish, Nova Scotia, but the MacDonalds and Syperek had been playing together for longer than that.

"Being from a town as small as Antigonish, where three of us were born and Sean was partially raised, made us practice a lot more than we might have if we had more things to do," says John-Angus. "From a very early age we played all the time in the garage and at house parties out of sheer boredom."

But for a band with serious career aspirations, Antigonish doesn't have much to offer. And John-Angus says the guys "were on a mission to make everybody hear us." The first step, one would think, would be to make a move to the nearby musical hotbed of Halifax. But the group didn't feel a part of that scene and elected to move to southern Ontario, which is much more densely populated and offers a lot more performance opportunities.

"We were aiming for Toronto, but missed it by an hour," jokes John-Angus about the band's move to Niagara Falls. Actually, they found rent much cheaper in the honeymoon capital; John-Angus had relatives there; and their manager at the time lived in nearby Buffalo, New York, so taking up residence in Niagara Falls made sense. John-Angus says they found "an incredibly cheap house where we all lived for a year and a half. We wrote all of the first album in the living room, and we named the album *House Of Ill Fame* after it."

After renaming themselves The Trews (a shortened form of Trousers in Scottish slang) when they found out that another group had already taken Trouser, the boys in the band set out to play as much as they could. John-Angus believes that their East

The Trews (L to R): Sean Dalton, Colin MacDonald, John-Angus MacDonald, Jack Syperek (2005)

BaNd tRiViA

Bassist Jack Syperek's father, Victor, is somewhat of a celebrity in his own right—both in and out of music circles. He's been a member of the VideoFACT board, which grants funds to Canadian artists to produce music videos. He owns Halifax's foremost live music club, The Marquee, as well as two popular restaurants in the city. And he finished second in his bid to become mayor of Halifax in 2004.

Coast roots had a huge influence on their outlook on their music. "I don't think that we were ever too pretentious or precious about music, because it was always something that people did at kitchen parties. It's never really been about stardom on the East Coast. You just play when you're happy or when you're sad, and you play for whoever's around who will listen."

And gradually, show by show, people began to listen. The band members became road warriors after *House Of Ill Fame* was released in August 2003 through manager Larry Wanagas' independent label, The Bumstead Recording Company. The label, in turn, signed a production and distribution deal with Sony Music Canada to get the album in stores across the country.

House Of Ill Fame was recorded at two Toronto studios and was produced by former Big Sugar frontman Gordie Johnson, who also played guitar and banjo on a few tracks. The disc featured 12 melodic rock songs that were influenced by such greats as Led Zeppelin, Aerosmith and The Rolling Stones. "Imagine Elvis Costello meeting AC/DC," is how John-Angus describes the band's sound, while his brother counters with, "It's like R.E.M. meets Aerosmith."

House Of Ill Fame ended up spawning four singles: "Every Inambition," "Fleeting Trust," "Tired Of Waiting," which used a bit of a reggae rhythm and is vaguely reminiscent of Led Zeppelin's "Your Time Is Gonna Come," and, most importantly, the relatively simple but rocking "Not Ready To Go." That song's catchy and singable chorus helped make it a number one Canadian rock radio hit, and it went on to become the most played single on domestic rock radio stations in 2004. The "Not Ready To Go" video also topped the MuchMoreMusic chart.

"We usually send the song to a bunch of directors, and then they come back with an array of treatments," John-Angus says of the group's approach to videos. "We know when we read it if the director gets the vibe of the song or if it's so mismatched that we think it's funny like the "Not Ready To Go" video. The band tends to think inside the box because it's so close to the song, so I like to hear a director's take on it. And if it has a creative hook and something that we think would be cool visually, then we go with it."

Sales started slowly, but *House Of Ill Fame's* momentum kept growing with each successive video, increased airplay and the almost non-stop gigs. The Trews headlined at smaller clubs and played in front of large arena audiences while opening for big acts including Evanescence, Nickelback and The Offspring.

Performing more than 400 shows in two years tightened the bonds between the band members even more, and it also helped them understand the music business better. While they had their ups and downs, and often felt drained both mentally and physically by being on the move all the time, they believe that it really strengthened their character.

"It's almost like an action movie," Colin MacDonald said in the October–November 2005 issue of *Access*. "Because you'll have a calm, and everything's cool, and then all of a sudden you round a corner and there's a blistering snowstorm, and you're stuck and you don't have chains for your tires."

The Trews received a 2004 Juno Award nomination for new group of the year, and *House Of Ill Fame* eventually sold more than 50,000 copies in Canada (the CD was reissued in November 2004 with a bonus live disc). All of the new experiences and that taste of success were bound to creep into the band's music when it came time to start thinking about its second CD. A lot of the tracks on the record were written and developed on the road at sound checks or in hotel rooms, while others came from jam sessions that the guys were able to fit in during their hectic touring schedule.

"I think on the first album we spent a lot of time not really knowing what to expect," Colin said in *Access*. "We were jamming in a living room; we were playing around Ontario; we were writing songs about being kind of young and confused. And this album is very much about human relations and growing as a person and realizing life on a grander perspective."

The Trews visited Johnson in his new hometown of Austin, Texas, in December 2004 to tinker with some songs, and the collaborative effort resulted in four tracks that would eventually make it to the new album. In January 2005, the band spent four days recording

demos in The Tragically Hip's Bathouse studio in Bath, Ontario. After that, it was time to start recording with Grammy Award-winning producer Jack Douglas, who had previously worked with the likes of The Who, John Lennon, Lou Reed and the New York Dolls.

"Jack is a legend who still has an edge," says Colin. "His unique, organic approach has captured the energy of our band perfectly. He allowed us the artistic freedom to bring our sound and performance to new levels."

The Trews recorded 20 songs for the album and chose 14 originals and a cover of Tracey Bonham's "Naked," which Douglas introduced to the band. They recorded each track—sometimes twice, sometimes 10 times—and then they chose the rendition that best captured the energy of the live show. The group followed the philosophy that the best take is not always the most perfect.

"If there's a drum screwup or a guitar string breaking, you just go ahead and keep that take. Because the most important thing about recorded music is to create somewhat of a moving experience, whether it's rockin' out, going crazy, having fun or feeling really sad, but you've got to capture that feeling," Colin told *Access.*

While still focusing on the raunchy rock-and-roll of the first album, *Den Of Thieves* added more obvious blues, soul and southern rock influences, while introducing horns on "Cry," a string section on "I Can't Say" and some mean harmonica from Big Sugar's Kelly Hoppe on "Got Myself to Blame."

"I think our new record is better than our first record because we were more comfortable in the studio and were better prepared," John-Angus says. "We've played so many shows that we're a great live band. There will come a point in our recording career that we've made so many records that we'll be an amazing recording band. But for the time being we just try to capture the energy of what we're about live."

Following a 2005 East Coast Music Award victory for group of the year and a Juno nomination for "Not Ready to Go" as single of the year, the anticipation for *Den Of Thieves* was palpable before its August 2005 release. The message board membership on The Trews' website grew and helped spread the word. "We sold more records in the first two weeks of this new one being out than we did in the first year of the last one," says John-Angus, who points out that *Den Of Thieves* was certified gold within a few months of its release on the strength of two singles and videos: "So She's Leaving" and "Yearning."

Since the band was relatively unknown when the first album came out, Sony didn't make it a major priority and The Trews sold a lot of copies of *House Of Ill Fame* at its shows. But as the momentum for that album kept building, so did the anticipation for its follow-up. But even the guys were caught by surprise when *Den Of Thieves* debuted at number six on the Canadian sales chart on its release.

The group members received another pleasant surprise in August. After the band members asked if Wanagas could get them tickets to The Rolling Stones' warm-up show at Toronto's Phoenix Concert Theatre before the Stones' 2005 world tour, their manager went one step further and landed The Trews the opening slot for the concert. "In the annals of our career, I don't know if we'll be able to top that, with it being a club show and it being the Stones," John-Angus said in a December 2, 2005 article on ChartAttack.com.

The Trews had another dream come true when the group was chosen to open for Led Zeppelin singer Robert Plant on his Canadian tour. For a band whose members vowed never to network

their way to the top, The Trews certainly found favor with a lot of influential people. "We never wanted to go out there and meet all the right guys and come up with the perfect band logo and get the right haircuts and everybody dress the same and invite the certain reps to your gigs," said Colin in a soundline.ca article.

> "We were like, let's just keep playing our asses off. We found a great manager who believed in the same thing we did, which is let's do this through the music. And we just let people come to us."

House Of Ill Fame wasn't released in the U.S., but *Den Of Thieves* was expected to come out there in the first quarter of 2006. The Trews had spent some time playing shows south of the border, but now want to focus more of their attention on the U.S. to support *Den Of Thieves*.

"The plan is to build it down there much the same way we built it up here—by being in people's faces and catching the buzz from town to town so that every time you come back there are more and more people," says John-Angus. "Playing live and touring are the only things in your hands. Otherwise you're relying on an industry that seems to be in a complete state of chaos right now."

Like the first album, the Bumstead Recording Company released *Den of Thieves*, but its master recordings were licensed to Sony BMG Music Entertainment. John-Angus says they have a good reputation with the multinational corporation, though he concedes that the music business is different in the U.S. than it is in Canada. But the guys are ready to roll out that road-hardened Canuck work ethic once again.

Since the U.S. is so much more densely populated than Canada, it's not as challenging to tour there. While it's a harder market to break into for Canadian bands, there are usually two- and three-hour drives between cities instead of the double-digit marathons that they're often faced with at home.

> The Trews know all too well what a big country Canada is, but they also think that the rest of the world is ready to hear their music. "You can only play this country so many times before people are going to be like, 'Yeah, it's good, but I just saw it five times last month,'" Colin explained in *Access*.

"You've got to respect that fact, that people are going to have already seen us 9 and 10 times last year. So we definitely want to move on to other territories so that we can keep what we have in Canada a special thing."

billy talent

Billy Talent was named after a character from Michael Turner's 1993 rock 'n' roll novel, *Hard Core Logo*. But the acclaim that has come the band's way since the 2003 release of its self-titled debut album has been anything but fictional.

The group members—singer Ben Kowalewicz, guitarist Ian D'Sa, bassist Jon Gallant and drummer Aaron Solowoniuk—met at a high school talent show in Mississauga, Ontario, in 1993. They soon formed a new band called Pezz and set up their own shows when they weren't attending school or working day jobs. They self-released their first full-length album, *Watoosh!* in 1998. The record mixed straight-up rock 'n' roll with punk, ska and metal. In combination with the band's high-energy live shows, the album helped Pezz start attracting attention outside of the group's circle of friends.

An American punk band also called Pezz found out about the Mississauga upstarts and threatened to sue them if they didn't change their name. That's when the group came up with the Billy Talent moniker. Shortly thereafter, they released the four-song *Try Honesty* EP and landed a deal with EMI Music Publishing Canada. Their shows got bigger, and radio programmers and major record companies began paying attention. In 2002, Billy Talent signed a joint deal with Warner Music Canada and Atlantic Records.

"When we were Pezz, we were trying so hard to satisfy every kind of genre that was out there at the time that we were missing the point," says Kowalewicz, who points out that the band has recently re-released *Watoosh!* on its own "to give us and everyone else a timeline and show them where things started."

2003

BaNd tRiViA
Singer Ben Kowalewicz enjoys cooking and says
he makes a really good chicken parmigiana.

Try Honesty was the title of the fiery first single from Billy Talent's punk-inspired first album, and it's also the approach that the group members have vowed to stick to as long as they're making music.

"For years we tried to find our sound, but everything started happening when we simply accepted what we are," says Kowalewicz. "When you find your voice, everything else follows suit."

The self-titled *Billy Talent* was produced by Gavin Brown, who has also worked with The Tea Party, Three Days Grace and Thornley. Its 13 tracks showed an impressive range of aural dynamics and tempos, and despite the aggression of the music and Kowalewicz's occasional screams used to punch up the passion in certain songs, the album was well-structured and full of hooky melodies.

On top of the solid musicianship, Kowalewicz's lyrics dealt with such topics as overcoming abuse, dealing with ridicule, coping with a friend's disease and facing up to painful recollections. "Most of my inspiration comes from listening to different people's experiences and points of view," says Kowalewicz, who often writes in the middle of the night when he can't sleep.

"Lyrics are about imagery, telling the story and expressing an emotion in which the music complements the words, and the words the music. My inspiration comes when I'm not comfortable, when I'm faced with situations and have to let everything out."

Young Canadians identified with what Billy Talent had to say and quickly made it one of the country's most popular bands through the help of four top-10 rock radio singles ("Try Honesty," "The Ex," "River Below" and "Nothing to Lose"). "Try Honesty" was voted best new single at the 2003 CASBY (Canadian Artists Selected By You) Awards, put on by influential Toronto radio station Edge 102 (where Kowalewicz once worked as a show producer). The video for the song took the rock title at the 2004 MuchMusic Video Awards, and Billy Talent was named best new group at the Juno Awards that same year.

When the band wasn't accepting awards, it was spreading its music across North America and around the globe by headlining its own shows, opening for such veteran bands as the Buzzcocks, and playing festivals like Lollapalooza and the Vans Warped Tour. Solowoniuk believes the band's live success comes from the members' philosophy that everything else is second to putting on a good show. Every performance is unique because the band members don't rehearse how the show will go, preferring to feed off each other and respond to the crowd.

Billy Talent tours almost non-stop, a strategy that provides a big boost to record sales and careers, but isn't always conducive to a stable personal life. "It's a double-edged sword," concedes Kowalewicz. "You don't ever want to complain because it's a dream come true and an opportunity that very few people get, and we're thankful. But as a human being, sometimes it's a grueling process. It can be tough sometimes being away from your loved ones. I've lost friends and girlfriends to being in the band, but I'm not going to trade it for anything."

Videos are important to Billy Talent, and the band likes to be heavily involved in coming up with concepts for them because Kowalewicz believes that "most rock videos today are pathetic." Their efforts paid off when the group won its second and third MuchMusic Video Awards in 2005 when "River Below" was named both best rock video and video of the year. The guys added those to the 2005 Junos that they won for group and album of the year.

Winning awards was the last thing that they were thinking about when they were slogging it out at basement rehearsals and during

Billy Talent (L to R): Jon Gallant, Ian D'Sa, Ben Kowalewicz, Aaron Solowoniuk (2003)

early shows in front of tiny crowds. Still, Kowalewicz concedes that it's nice to be recognized for all of the hard work they've put in and the sacrifices they've made to get to this point.

> "But once you start caring too much about that and you start worrying about that kind of stuff, that's where you can get shot in the foot. It's nice for the parents. It's flattering."

What means more to Billy Talent, Kowalewicz insists, is making an impact on other people's lives with its music. When "Nothing to Lose" was released as a single and video, the band pledged to donate a dollar to the Kids Help Phone every time a Canadian radio or video outlet played it. It ended up contributing more than $3500 to helping teens in crisis. The group thought the song's theme was a perfect fit with the organization's purpose.

Kowalewicz says of the idea's genesis, "We came up with a concept and called Kids Help Phone, and they were all on board. We became ambassadors for the hotline, which was kind of cool. We've heard that people have called and asked for help because of the video. That's a pretty amazing thing.

"It's just rock 'n' roll music, but sometimes it can really help people out. It was something that we really enjoyed doing, and I think on the next record we're going to do something else for something that's affected the band."

Billy Talent has sold almost 300,000 copies in Canada and around 100,000 more south of the border. After the first record's success, it was time to write and record what is often referred to in the music industry as the "difficult" second album. But the band members elected not to rush into the studio because they wanted to make sure that they felt totally happy with the songs before recording them with Brown. Besides, Kowalewicz says that he's a live performer who would much rather be on a stage than in the studio. "I hate the studio more than anything. I like the end result and being there and witnessing everyone else doing their stuff. But when it's my turn, I hate it."

Kowalewicz admits, however, that putting in time in the studio has helped make him a better singer. And he's excited about the new album and the improved sound and songwriting that he says fans can expect. "The sound of the last record was okay, but it was pretty processed. This one's a little bit more raw, and a little louder and a little more rocky. I think it's better in every way, shape and form. I'm just so stoked to be getting it out to people."

Aside from anticipating a late spring or early summer release for the album, and subsequent Warped Tour and European festival dates, Kowalewicz likes to take things day by day and is reluctant to look too far into the future. He hopes the group's members can just keep doing what they love, and that people will keep listening. "We'll continue going until it's irrelevant and it's sort of reached its end."

Kowalewicz is a proud Canadian, as he proclaims from the stage during every show, and he's particularly proud of how buoyant the Canadian music scene has been in the past few years. "I think that the best bands in the world right now are coming out of our country," he declares.

"One thing I like about being Canadian is that I can go and hang out with k-os, and then I can bump into Kevin Drew from Broken Social Scene, and I can see the guys from Hot Hot Heat and the guys from Sum 41, and everyone's cool with each other. Stylistically and musically, we're all very different bands, but everyone fights the same fight from a different angle and from a different tactical position."

matt mays & el torpedo

Matt Mays first came to the attention of music fans as a 19-year-old who joined The Guthries, a Dartmouth, Nova Scotia alternative country band with rock and pop influences. The group released the critically acclaimed *Off Windmill* debut album in 2000, toured across Canada and Europe, and received a 2001 Canadian Country Music Award nomination for roots artist of the year. While the band was recording the self-titled follow-up, the founding members parted company with Mays.

"We started doing the second record, and it was a fun record to make," Mays says. "But I started working on a solo record at the same time because there were four songwriters in the band."

Mays didn't plan to launch a solo career with the release, but he discovered that he enjoyed the freedom of being able to record all of his songs and to lead the direction of the album.

"I didn't leave the band, I was sort of asked to leave the band, which is kind of a common misunderstanding," says Mays. "I understood because there was a bit of friction because I was so into my own thing."

While Mays and the members of The Guthries have put their differences behind them and play on each other's records, the career of the lanky Hamilton, Ontario-born singer/songwriter and guitarist has clearly been on the rise since the split. "I've learned a lot about songwriting because I do it all the time," he says of his evolution since striking out on his own.

Matt Mays was released in 2003 under licence to Sonic Records, the label run by Mays' manager, Louis Thomas. Sonic, in turn, is distributed across the country by Warner Music Canada. The

10-song CD, featuring artwork by Mays' father Bill, is a melodic, rootsy pop-rock album that showcases his talent as a songwriter. The disc spawned the singles "Where Am I Going?" and the more popular "City of Lakes."

While the album was just called *Matt Mays*, its sound was filled out by musical contributions from Blue Rodeo's Bob Egan, members of The Guthries and the young men who would eventually become his full-time band.

"I consider my first record a good transition between what I was doing with The Guthries and what I'm doing now with El Torpedo," explains Mays. "When those guys played on the first record, they weren't called El Torpedo. They were just my buddies. But

Matt Mays (2005)

BaNd tRiViA

The band does some fancy line-dancing steps in the video for "On The Hood." The choreographer for the routine was Cory Bowles, a member of the '90s East Coast hip-hop group Hip Club Groove. He's now better known as Cory from the television show *Trailer Park Boys*.

eventually, when the record was released, they were. At the time, I didn't know what kind of a live band we would turn out to be."

El Torpedo turned out to be a band that rocked much harder than a listen to the first album would have you believe. Constant touring back and forth across Canada—playing headline shows in small clubs and opening for acts like Blue Rodeo and Sam Roberts in larger venues—made the band members into an even more cohesive unit than when they first set out from Dartmouth.

"We all grew up in close families and had wholesome values from the ground up," emphasizes Mays, who believes those roots have influenced how the band members treat each other, especially on tour. "We have a lot of respect for each other, like a family."

Aside from Matt Mays, El Torpedo includes bassist Andy Patil, guitarist Jarrett Murphy and drummer Tim Baker. Former member Brad Conrad—who played organ, guitar and pedal steel—left the band in the summer of 2005 and was replaced by Rob Crowell.

"The first rule of this band is that if you have something on your mind, you say it," Mays stresses. "If you start holding grudges, it can become a serious problem. We have to keep everything on the table, and the best way to solve things is to get it out."

Matt Mays and El Torpedo was given the Galaxie Rising Star Award and $3000 for being named the favorite act at the 2003 North By Northeast Music Festival in Toronto. Mays continued his winning ways by taking the new artist of the year title at the 2004 East Coast Music Awards in St. John's, Newfoundland. He was also nominated for a 2005 best new artist Juno, while the debut recording earned a Juno nod for adult alternative album of the year.

Mays was supposed to have met Neil Young, one of his idols, at the Juno ceremony in Winnipeg. Sadly, a brain aneurysm prevented the living legend from making the trip and, perhaps, from passing his ragged rock torch on to Mays—who has drawn numerous comparisons to both Young and Tom Petty.

"A lot of people see more of the Neil Young influence because it's more visible, but I personally feel that I'm more influenced by Bob Dylan than Neil Young," says Mays. "When I was learning how to write songs, all I was listening to was Bob Dylan, Neil Young, Tom Petty and Gordon Lightfoot—guys that write three-chord songs with lyrics that punch you in the face and hit you in the heart."

The second album was recorded between the Sonic Temple and Ultramagnetic Recording studios in Halifax, and 11 of its 14 songs were produced by Grammy Award winner Don Smith, whose impressive resumé includes work with The Rolling Stones, The Tragically Hip and, quite appropriately, Bob Dylan and Tom Petty. The group liked Smith's reputation for capturing live performances in the studio, and Mays was thrilled when the producer agreed to come to Halifax along with some of his vintage guitars and recording equipment.

> "He was all about the vibe we had," says Mays of Smith. "If a take had a lot of mojo and some mistakes, we'd keep that one over a perfect take."

Matt Mays and El Torpedo, which again featured the art of Bill Mays on the cover, was released by Sonic and Warner in March 2005. "On the second record we wanted to draw attention to the fact that we are a band," says Mays, who emphasizes that, although he writes the lyrics and comes up with the ideas for the songs, the final product is often derived from jams involving the whole group.

"Cocaine Cowgirl," the guitar-heavy first single and video, was the most added rock song at Canadian radio stations in its first week of release and went on to become a major hit. It was followed by "On The Hood," a mid-tempo number that mixes acoustic and electric guitars and sounds a bit reminiscent of George Harrison. Kathleen Edwards, who contributed vocals to "The Plan," was one of the album's guest performers.

"It's about as primitive and honest as a record can be," said Mays of the album in the June 2005 issue of *Progress*. "Nothing is fabricated, everything is live, off the floor. It was important for us to keep it as old-style as possible."

Matt Mays and El Torpedo once again traversed Canada, playing to larger crowds this time, and went to England for a brief tour with Blue Rodeo. The band went to Germany to support the January release of the album there, and the members are looking to land deals in the UK and U.S. so that they can spend more time in those territories.

"Until that happens, we'll play a few showcase gigs—like South by Southwest—to stir up some interest," Mays said in the March 24, 2005 issue of *NOW Magazine*. "The main thing we need to do right now is get in front of people, because performing is really our strength. I think things just make more sense to people once they've seen us."

Matt Mays & El Torpedo (L to R): Andy Patil, Rob Crowell, Tim Jim Baker, Jarett Murphy, Matt Mays (2005)

While audience response in countries other than Canada has been enthusiastic, Mays believes that he's following a path similar to such quintessentially Canadian acts as Gordon Lightfoot, Blue Rodeo and The Tragically Hip.

"There's the honesty of Canadians and the down-home, down-to-earth friendliness that comes into play," Mays says. "The space and vast horizons and unpopulated spaces are what I hear. Canadian music has a wholesome honesty to it that's apparent and audible to me."

Mays and El Torpedo are already tinkering with songs for their next album. While there won't be any drastic changes, Mays says there will be more precision in the song arrangements.

> "It's like a baby born with an IQ of 110 and is able to speak already. The songs are coming out of us pre-arranged."

Mays has also been working on another solo record that he says is "quite a bit different" from what he's doing with El Torpedo, and he hopes to get it into people's hands soon.

"I don't want to be one of those guys who releases a record every three years," he emphasizes. "I want to have a lot of records. As an artist, I'd rather have a bunch of paintings to my name rather than just a couple of intricate ones."

Mays is one of those people who just can't stay still, which is why movement and traveling are such predominant themes in his music. If he's not in a van driving to his next gig, he's probably back in Dartmouth or Halifax puttering around a studio. And if you can't find him in either of those places, look towards the nearest body of water that has large waves.

"Surfing's kind of my first love," Mays conceded in the April 4, 2005 issue of *Maclean's*. "There's no strings attached, just the board and ocean. Music's great, but lots of crap goes along with it."

alexisonfire

Alexisonfire has accomplished a lot more than it expected since releasing its self-titled debut album in 2002, but the St. Catharines, Ontario heavy rock quintet wants its fans to know that becoming wealthy isn't one of them.

"Because we get so much video play and have hosted shows on MuchMusic, there's more of a perception of celebrity," says guitarist and vocalist Wade MacNeil. "People probably assume that we're extremely rich because they see us on television, which is not the case."

But even if mass riches haven't yet come the band's way, adulation, a Canadian gold record, global album sales of more than 200,000 and opportunities to travel around the world certainly have. Not too shabby for a group that still had members in high school when its first record came out.

Wade MacNeil, Chris Steele (bass), Dallas Green (guitar and vocals) and Jesse Ingelevics (drums) all grew up in St. Catharines, while singer and screamer George Petit is from the nearby Niagara region town of Grimsby. All of them got to know each other either through school or a shared interest in music. "The fact that we're from a smaller city probably made us a lot more interested in music because there's not tons to do in a city like St. Catharines," MacNeil explains.

Alexisonfire took its name from Alexis Fire, an adult film actress. The band burst on to the scene with its debut, which was the first release on the independent Distort Entertainment label. While both the band and the label were essentially newbies to the business, everyone involved worked hard, and Alexisonfire quickly established a strong bond with its fans through its frenetic live

Alexisonfire (L to R): Jordan Hastings, Chris Steele, Wade MacNeil, Dallas Green, George Petit (2005)

shows across the country. The tour helped spread the word and sell some albums, but things really started to take off when Much-Music stepped in with support. MacNeil credits MuchMusic with helping to jump-start the band's popularity in Canada.

Videos for lead singles "Pulmonary Archery," "Counterparts and Number Them" and "Waterwings" were all put into heavy rotation on MuchMusic and MuchLoud, and "Counterparts" received the VideoFACT Award at the 2004 MuchMusic Video Awards. The band members are involved in developing concepts for their videos and feel that it's important to come up with something interesting and different. They also use videos to try and convey their sense of humor, something that's usually in short supply in the often dark and ominous extreme "screamo" music genre that Alexisonfire often gets lumped in with.

> "I like metal as much as everyone else, but we're not that kind of band," Green told *Chart* in its July–August 2004 issue. "We don't want to be fake. We're having fun!"

The screaming, courtesy of Petit, separates Alexisonfire from other groups. But the man who also writes many of the group's lyrics doesn't do it out of anger, he insists. That aspect of the group's sound, which has forced Petit to see a throat specialist for the damage caused by over-exerting his vocal chords night after night, merely acts as a unique counterpoint to Green's singing and the band's more melodic moments.

The group's energy and constant onstage movement, which have helped draw the band's legion of fans, haven't come without a cost.

Every member has been injured in one way or another, with cuts, bruises and fractures relatively commonplace. But seeing musicians put so much into their show that they bleed on stage can have a real impact on a young music lover, and it has helped solidify the close bonds between Alexisonfire and its followers. And because many of its fans are below the age of majority, the band tries to stay out of licensed venues and play as many all-ages shows as it possibly can.

"I think when we came out, kids saw honesty," Green said in the spring 2005 issue of *Words and Music*. "They saw we were just like them—a bunch of kids trying their hardest—and they just got behind us. Some kids have told us that we've saved their lives, and that's the best compliment ever."

MacNeil says that the band members try and keep in touch with people who write to them, and they'll often walk around in the audience to talk to fans at gigs. They avoid erecting security barriers at their shows so crowd members can get up close and even stage-dive if it's safe.

This fan-friendly philosophy has paid off, and many supporters have shown their devotion by emulating MacNeil and Green and

2005

getting the Alexisonfire logo tattooed on their bodies. MacNeil doesn't know exactly how many people have done this, but judging by those he's seen in person and has viewed in photos, he thinks that it could be in the hundreds. To show its appreciation, the band has instituted a policy forever welcoming anyone with an Alexisonfire tattoo into every concert for free.

Alexisonfire toured across Canada and the U.S. (where it has a deal with Equal Vision Records) in support of the first album, and the band built such a solid fan base that its *Watch Out!* follow-up debuted at number six on the Canadian sales chart in June 2004. That's an amazing accomplishment for a young group on an independent label like Distort, although the label does have major record company distribution through Universal Music Canada after moving from EMI Music Canada.

Watch Out! was also released in Europe, Japan and Australia through different indie labels, which MacNeil says the band is quite pleased with. Despite the band's growing success, he sees no need to jump to a major label.

"We're not necessarily opposed to signing with a major label, but now definitely would not be the time to do it," MacNeil says. "We just need to be on a label that cares about us and wants to push us and wants to work the band as hard as we want to work it."

The band members all felt that they succeeded in topping their debut with *Watch Out!* Their previous studio experience and extensive touring since the release of the first record gave them the confidence to try new things. This resulted in a more polished album that relied less on the screaming and more on Green's emotive vocals, as well as more emphasis on melody and dynamic tension. The heavy parts were heavier, while the soft parts were softer.

Twelve weeks after *Watch Out!*'s release, the album received a gold certification for selling 50,000 copies in Canada. While radio support was still lacking, Much once again came on board to play the videos for "Accidents," "No Transitory" and "Hey, It's Your Funeral Mama." Alexisonfire performed at the 2005 MuchMusic Video Awards along with the Black Eyed Peas, the Killers and Ashlee Simpson, and "Accidents" was named best independent video. The band received an even bigger honor in April 2005 when it won the prize for new group of the year at the Juno Awards in Winnipeg.

Despite having so much success in such a relatively short time, the band members have been careful to make sure that no swelled heads get in the way. Their close friendships make it easy for them to be open and honest with each other, and their fun-loving attitude towards both life and their music has also helped.

Alexisonfire's international profile increased as it undertook major tours in the U.S., Japan, Australia, Europe and South America, playing more than 200 shows in support of *Watch Out!* MacNeil calls being on the road all the time a "bizarre and very unconventional way of living" that carries both extreme highs and lows. But the good parts make everything worth it, he insists. The members' experiences have made them more mature, and

2005

they've learned a lot about people. "You get put into a lot of situations that you have to react to, which help you grow up a little bit quicker," MacNeil explains.

The road seemed to take its toll on Ingelevics, however, who left the band in the middle of a tour to deal with personal issues. Drummer Jordan Hastings, a friend of the band from his time playing with former tourmate Jersey, replaced Inglevics.

Although the group doesn't talk too much about the former drummer's departure, the members posted a statement on the band's website on June 17, 2005: "Over the past few months on the road, things just grew apart—things just happened. Life just takes a weird course sometimes. We still love Jesse, and he is our friend. I know you're all looking for some specific, definitive moment when things came to a head, but sorry to say, it doesn't exist. There was no dramatic fight, no drug problems, no major moments—none of that typical rock-bullsh**."

MacNeil wants to release as much music as possible, so Alexisonfire and fellow rising Canadian rock band Moneen teamed up to release the six-song *The Switcheroo Series* EP in October 2005. The disc features a new song by each group and Alexisonfire covering Moneen's "Passing of America" and "Tonight I'm Gone,"

with Moneen covering Alexisonfire's "Sharks and Danger" and "Accidents."

"It's something cool for people who are into both bands," says MacNeil. "We're really stoked about the way they did our stuff, and they're happy with the way we interpreted their songs."

After wrapping up an American tour in November 2005, Alexisonfire started writing songs for its next album. The group planned to start recording in February, with the hope of having a late spring release.

> Julius Butty, who helped Alexisonfire produce *Watch Out!* will once again be back at the helm for the new album. MacNeil says the band members liked his work on the last album and wanted to work with him again.

Alexisonfire members are also involved with other projects during those rare moments of down time. Green works on his solo acoustic material under the moniker City and Colour and has released an album called *Sometimes*. Petit and MacNeil formed the Black Lungs with two members of Jersey and planned to release an album of what MacNeil calls "wimpy punk rock." But he emphasizes that Alexisonfire will always be their priority.

"We're all doing our side projects and stuff like that. But when we all play together the way that we should, it's definitely a hell of a lot better than any of that. There's something about the five of us playing together that's great and something special. Hopefully that doesn't have to end, and I don't really see why it would."

chapter fifteen

broken social scene

In 1999, Broken Social Scene was born with a musical meeting of the minds between Toronto musicians Kevin Drew and Brendan Canning.

Drew and Charles Spearin (Do Make Say Think) comprised a duo called K.C. Accidental. Canning had played bass with hHead, Len and By Divine Right and was also an active club DJ. The two men realized that they were on the same musical wavelength and started working together under the Broken Social Scene banner. Appropriately enough, their first performance took place at Toronto club Ted's Wrecking Yard on December 17, 2000, as part of the weekly Wavelength music series.

That winter Drew and Canning recorded the first Broken Social Scene album, the largely instrumental *Feel Good Lost*, with contributions from singer Leslie Feist (who had been in By Divine Right with Canning), drummer Justin Peroff and Evan Cranley (a member of Stars). The first full-band performance was on January 26, 2001 with Drew, Canning, Feist, Peroff and guitarist Andrew Whiteman (who's known in another incarnation as Apostle of Hustle). *Feel Good Lost* was released the next month.

Drew, Canning, Spearin, Peroff and Whiteman formed the core of Broken Social Scene, with Feist, Cranley, John Crossingham (Raising the Fawn), Bill Priddle (Treble Charger), Emily Haines (Metric) and James Shaw (Metric) joining them for performances whenever their schedules would allow it. The group's repertoire was all over the place and would often include ambient, dub, psychedelic, soul and noise-rock elements. Despite all of these apparent inconsistencies, Broken Social Scene developed a loyal following.

Producer Dave Newfeld's Stars and Sons studio hosted all of these people whenever they were able to assemble in one combination or another from the winter of 2001 through the summer of 2002. It wasn't the easiest way to record an album, but somehow all of the disparate parts were combined into a workable entity that was released in October 2002 under the title *You Forgot It in People*. The album was released jointly by Toronto independent label Paper Bag Records and Arts and Crafts—a new company created by Drew, his former roommate Jeffrey Remedios (who was working at Virgin Music Canada at the time) and another Virgin staffer, Daniel Cutler.

"As I got to know Kevin and Brendan and all these people around them, I was like, 'My God, you guys are at the centre of this artistic community of all these people,'" Remedios said in an October 15, 2005 article in the *Toronto Star*. "'If you guys came together in name, wouldn't that be a wonderful thing? It would be like a little miniature Group of Seven or something like that.'"

The sprawling yet cohesive *You Forgot It in People* sold out its initial 1000 copies within a month, and Broken Social Scene broke off its relationship with Paper Bag to focus on an expanding Arts and Crafts empire once Remedios and Cutler left Virgin. The label signed a Canadian distribution deal with EMI Music Canada and a similar pact in the U.S. with Caroline. Intense Internet chatter and rave reviews for the spacey but melodic CD spread the word

Broken Social Scene (L to R): Kevin Drew, Leslie Feist, Charles Spearin, Andrew Whiteman, Jason Collett, Justin Peroff, Brendan Canning (2003)

further, and Broken Social Scene soon found itself in demand across Canada.

"*You Forgot It in People* was an infection with a purpose," says Drew. "We made that record with determination to try something different. Something different from what we were doing in the past. Pop music was a sarcastic wonder to many of us, so it was obvious that something was going to happen. These songs infected the lives of those who wrote them and those lives affected the songs. Everyone got involved in different ways, and we became a band."

Toronto singer, songwriter and guitarist Jason Collett joined the group's core lineup, and the band was able to enlist the services of Cranley, Seligman, Amy Millan and Torquil Campbell while on one of its frequent tours with Stars. The group coordinated schedules with Feist and Metric in order to involve them as much as possible, too.

"I don't see us following any indie-rock handbook, really," Drew said about the band having to cope with its unusual make-up in an article in the September 3, 2004 issue of *Filter*. "I don't have the indie-rock handbook with me, and I've never read it anyway. I know it's wrong to turn on the television and hear your favorite song supporting toothpaste. And I know it's wrong to go on tour with Blink 182."

You Forgot It in People won the 2003 Juno Award for best alternative album, and the record earned accolades from high-profile magazines such as *Rolling Stone* and *SPIN* when the disc was released south of the border that June. Broken Social Scene played sold-out venues across the U.S. and eventually became a main act at European music festivals. While the constant touring helped

Broken Social Scene sell records—*You Forgot It in People* has sold more than 150,000 copies around the world—and climb a number of rungs up the indie rock ladder, it was also physically and mentally draining at times.

"Just because you're a band doesn't mean you should be in a tour bus touring," Canning said in an August 24, 2005 MTV.com article. "It's fairly archaic, and there's a reason why someone like Tom Waits doesn't tour very much: It's slightly uncivilized."

If you didn't see Broken Social Scene in person, you might have caught it occasionally on television. Drew and filmmaker George Vale made six videos for songs from *You Forgot It in People*, and "Stars and Sons" received a 2004 Juno nomination for best video.

While all of this was going on with Broken Social Scene, Arts and Crafts was also releasing records from the group's individual members, including Feist, Collett, Apostle of Hustle and Stars.

"All of our acts pretty much have come from attrition—if you're going to start a label, I highly recommend you start it with Broken Social Scene as your first band," Remedios said in the October 15 edition of the *Toronto Star*. "We put out 10 records without ever leaving the family."

Broken Social Scene's *Bee Hives*—a collection of older, previously unreleased material and some 2003 UK-only B-sides—was issued on March 18, 2004. "We chose these songs because of the calm nature that seemed to thread it all together. We found very few rockin' numbers but, instead, many songs for the come down," says Drew.

Broken Social Scene's members composed the score for the Bruce McDonald-directed film *The Love Crimes of Gillian Guess* that summer. The movie—which starred Joely Collins, the daughter of music legend Phil Collins, and former Headstones frontman Hugh Dillon—received a limited release.

> While *Bee Hives* kept fans satisfied for a while, Broken Social Scene worked on its next album in fits and spurts between tours and its members' other musical and non-musical obligations. The sessions went on constantly, as the group had no set recording schedule. Members came and went as they had time.

Newfeld was enlisted to produce Broken Social Scene's self-titled album at Stars and Sons, and he estimated that there were about 30 songs that had the potential to be on it. "This is really Newf's album," Drew said in a November 21, 2005 pitchforkmedia.com interview.

"He'd be up into all hours, and we'd be on tour and would say, 'Okay, Newf, since you've…taken over all this sh**, can you please finish the record while we're gone?' And we get back and he says, 'Well, I didn't finish the record, but listen to what I did to this tune!' And suddenly, a song you thought you knew has turned into a remix record or something."

When *Broken Social Scene* was released on October 4, 2005, the credits listed 17 people as members of the group. Violinist Julie Penner, Jason Tait (The Weakerthans), Murray Lightburn (The Dears) and organic hip-hop artist k-os were cited as guests. But since so many band members also have their own projects, and Drew and Canning were primarily concerned with Broken Social Scene, the pair have the biggest voice in what the collective ultimately sounds like.

The seven-song, 26-minute, limited-edition *EP To Be You and Me* was included with the initial manufacturing run of *Broken Social Scene*. The material is more direct than that found on the album, and the EP features a faster, countrified version of the *Broken Social Scene* track "Major Label Debut."

Despite all the ups and downs in making *Broken Social Scene*, Drew eventually came to love the album. "I think it's a big, gigantic, beautiful mess," he said in the pitchforkmedia.com interview.

"We never really followed any guidelines on how we did things, but in the end it's more of an indie rock record than we ever thought we'd make. It's really an indie rock record through and through, and it's an experimental psychedelic record, and all the chances and craziness and all the rules we broke are only going to help us in the long run. I think this record is going to make more sense in years to come than right now, but I have a lot of respect for the risks we took."

Canning is also pleased with how the eclectic *Broken Social Scene* turned out. "It's a barrage and collage of a lot of different sounds," he told the *Winnipeg Sun* in a November 17, 2005 article.

"It's not as innocent sounding a recording as *You Forgot It in People*. A couple of years of living a slightly different life has led this album down the path it's led."

Since there was so much music recorded for *Broken Social Scene*, there's lots of material available for another album. Drew and Canning plan on revisiting some of the demos and rough mixes and anticipate releasing a new Broken Social Scene record by the end of 2006. Fans will no doubt thank them for keeping the wait to a minimum this time around.

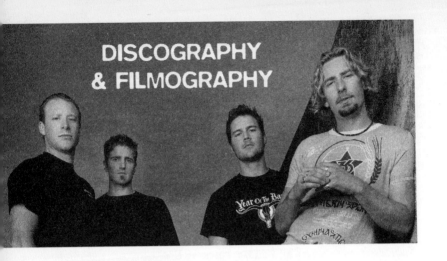

DISCOGRAPHY & FILMOGRAPHY

Nickelback

Albums

All the Right Reasons (2005)

The Long Road (2003)

Silver Side Up (2001)

The State (1999)

Curb (1996)

Hesher EP (1996)

DVDs

The Road to Success (2004)

The Videos (2003, re-released with bonus tracks 2004)

Live at Home (2002)

Sum 41

Albums

Go Chuck Yourself (2006)

Chuck (2004)

Maximum (interview album, 2003)

Does This Look Infected? (2002)

All Killer no Filler (2001)

Half Hour of Power (2000)

DVDs

Rocked: Sum 41 in the Congo (2005)

Bring the Noise (2004)

Sake Bombs and Happy Endings (2003)

Introduction to Destruction (2002)

Metric

Albums

Mainstream EP (1998)

Grow Up and Blow Away
  (officially unreleased, 2001)

Static Anonymity EP (2001)

Old World Underground,
  Where Are You Now? (2003)

Live It Out (2005)

Films

Clean (2004)

Our Lady Peace

Albums

Healthy In Paranoid Times (2005)

Live (2003)

Gravity (2002)

Spiritual Machines (2000)

Happiness Is Not a Fish That You Can Catch (1999)

Clumsy (1997)

Naveed (1994)

DVDs

Live (2003)

Hot Hot Heat

Albums

Elevator (2005)

Make Up the Breakdown (2002)

Knock Knock Knock EP (2002)

Scenes One Through Thirteen (2003)

Split (with Red Light Sting, 2000)

Simple Plan

Albums
MTV Hard Rock Live (2005)
Still Not Getting Any... (2004)
No Pads, No Helmets...Just Balls (2002)

DVDs
A Big Package For You (2003)

Films
New York Minute (2004)

The Tragically Hip

Albums
Yer Favorites (two-CD set, 2005)
In Between Evolution (2004)
In Violet Light (2002)
Music @ Work (2000)
Phantom Power (1998)
Live Between Us (1997)
Trouble at the Henhouse (1996)
Day for Night (1994)
Fully Completely (1992)

Road Apples (1991)

Up To Here (1989)

The Tragically Hip EP
(1987, re-mastered release 1989)

DVDs/Videos

Hipeponymous (two DVDs packed with
Yer Favorites two-CD set, 2005)

That Night in Toronto (2004)

Heksenketel (VHS documentary, 1998)

Films

Men With Brooms (2002)

Arcade Fire

Albums

Arcade Fire EP (2003)

Funeral (2004)

DVDs

Rebellion (Lies) (DVD single, 2005)

Default

Albums

One Thing Remains (2005)

Elocation (2003)

The Fallout (2001, re-released with
  bonus tracks and DVD, 2002)

The New Pornographers

Albums

Twin Cinema (2005)

Electric Version (2003)

Mass Romantic (2000)

The Trews

Albums

Den of Thieves (2005)

House of Ill Fame (2003, special edition re-release 2004)

Every Inambition EP (2003)

The Trews (2002)

Billy Talent

Albums

Billy Talent (2003)

Try Honesty EP (2001)

Watoosh!
  (as Pezz, 1998, re-released 2005)

DVDs

Scandalous Travelers (2004)

Matt Mays and El Torpedo

Albums

Matt Mays and El Torpedo (2005)

Matt Mays (2003)

Alexisonfire

Albums

The Switcheroo Series EP
  (with Moneen, 2005)

Watch Out! (2004)

Alexisonfire (2003)

Broken Social Scene

Albums

EP To Be You and Me (2005)
Broken Social Scene (2005)
Bee Hives (2004)
You Forgot It in People (2002)
Feel Good Lost (2001)

Notes on Sources

ALEXISONFIRE
Articles
Carman, Keith. "Alexisonfire: The Real Deal," *Chart*, Toronto, ON,
    July/August 2004
Krewen, Nick. "Alexisonfire: The Sultans of Scream-o Rock On," *Words &
    Music*, Toronto, ON, Spring 2005.

ARCADE FIRE
Articles
Barclay, Michael. "Arcade Fire Talk about the Passion," *Exclaim!*, Toronto, ON,
    September 2004.
Hilburn, Robert. "Riding the Tide," *Los Angeles Times*, Los Angeles, CA,
    January 16, 2005.
Hoard, Christian. "The Fire this Time," *Rolling Stone*, New York, NY,
    March 10, 2005.
Liss, Sarah. "The Arcade Fire," *NOW Magazine*, Toronto, ON, June 17, 2004.
Mills, Fred. "View at the Top," *Magnet Magazine*, Philadelphia, PA,
    April/May 2005.
Web Articles
Heraclitus. "Heraclitus Sayz Interview: Arcade Fire, "
    http://www.heraclitussayz.com/hcsayz-int-arcadefire.htm
Perez, Rodrigo. "Arcade Fire Hiding in Plain Sight with New Single, Fall Tour,"
    http://www.mtv.com/news/articles/1505916/20050718/story.jhtml,
    July 18, 2005.
Schreiber, Ryan. "Interview: The Arcade Fire,"
    http://www.pitchforkmedia.com/interviews/a/arcade-fire-05/index3.shtml,
    February 14, 2005.
Warner, Tyrone. "The Arcade Fire Burning the Midnight Oil,"
    http://www.tinymixtapes.com/interviews/arcade_fire2.htm, October 2004.
Web Resources
http://en.wikipedia.org/wiki/Arcade_Fire

BROKEN SOCIAL SCENE
Articles
Leckart, Steve. "Getting to Know Broken Social Scene," *Filter Magazine*, Los
    Angeles, CA, September 3, 2004.
Siddiqui, Tabassum. "All in the Family," *Toronto Star*, Toronto, ON,
    October 15, 2005.
Williams, Rob. "Broken Social Scene Leads Canuck Rock," *Winnipeg Sun*,
    Winnipeg, MB, November 17, 2005.
Web Articles
Borzykowski, Bryan. "Broken Social Scene Ready Three Records, K-OS
    Contributing," http://www.chartattack.com/DAMN/2005/04/1507.cfm,
    April 15, 2005.

Perez, Rodrigo. "Broken Social Scene's Agenda: Two LPs, Touring, Hating on Audioslave,"
http://www.mtv.com/news/articles/1508297/20050824/story.jhtml,
August 24, 2005.

Schreiber, Ryan. "Interview: Broken Social Scene,"
http://pitchforkmedia.com/interviews/b/broken-social-scene-05,
November 21, 2005.

DEFAULT
Articles
McConvey, Joel. "Default Tugging at Heartstrings," *Chart*, Toronto, ON, December 2003/January 2004.
Web Articles
LochnessPimpster, "Default," http://www.smother.net/interviews/default.php3.
Sculley, Alan. "Default's Future Depends on 'One Thing,'" www.flipsidepa.com.

HOT HOT HEAT
Web Articles
Keene, Darrin. "Hot Hot Heat Defy the Comparisons,"
http://www.chartattack.com/DAMN/2002/11/0608.cfm, November 6, 2002.

MATT MAYS & EL TORPEDO
Articles
Deziel, Shanda. "Matt Mays & El Torpedo Promise Soul and a Whole Lot of Mojo," *Maclean's Magazine*, Toronto, ON, April 4, 2005.
Fletcher-Naylor, Corrie. "[the artist]," *Progress*, Halifax, NS, June 2005.
Perlich, Tim. "Matt Mays & El Torpedo," *NOW Magazine*, Toronto, ON, March 24, 2005.

METRIC
Articles
Borzykowski, Bryan. "Metric Fight the War," *Chart*, Toronto, ON, November 2005.
Redfern, Mark. "Metric," *Under The Radar*, Beverly Hills, CA, Fall 2005.
Shaw, James. "Metric: The Tour Diary," *Toronto Star*, Toronto, ON, November 6, 2005.
Wheeler, Brad. "Metric Goes the Distance," The Globe and Mail, Toronto, ON, September 23, 2005.
Web Articles
Borzykowski, Bryan. "Metric Grow Up and Live It Out,"
http://www.chartattack.com/DAMN/2005/10/2811.cfm, October 28, 2005.
Carlson, Jan. "The Gothamist Band Interview: Metric,"
http://www.gothamist.com/archives/2005/10/05/the_gothamist_band_inter
view_metric.php, October 5, 2005.

THE NEW PORNOGRAPHERS
Articles
Borzykowski, Bryan. "The New Pornographers Defy Distance," *Chart*, Toronto, ON, September 2005.

Bruno, Franklin. "Mass Appeal: Canuck Collective the New Pornographers Serve Up a Second Helping," Seattle Weekly, Seattle, WA, June 11, 2003.

Web Articles
Perez, Rodrigo. "Pornographers' Cinema No Dirty Little Secret," http://www.mtv.com/news/articles/1513426/20051110/story.jhtml, November 10, 2005.

NICKELBACK
Articles
Devlin, Mike. "Rock Revival," *Victoria Times Colonist*, Victoria, BC, January 15, 2002.

Krewen, Nick. "Nickelback Finds Gold in the Dark," *Nightlife*, Kitchener, ON, February 12, 2004.

Pascual, Brian. "Nickelback Break Up the Family," *Chart*, Toronto, ON, October 2005.

Rayner, Ben. "Top of the Game," *Toronto Star*, Toronto, ON, February 5, 2004.

Ross, Mike. "Fired Nickelback Member 'Betrayed,'" *The Edmonton Sun*, Edmonton, AB, January 28, 2005.

Ross, Mike. "The Nickelbacklash," *The Edmonton Sun*, Edmonton, AB, January 25, 2004.

Smiderle, Wes. "Getting the Hang of the Big Time," *The Ottawa Citizen*, Ottawa, ON, December 9, 1999.

Smiderle, Wes. "Silver Side Up. Way Up: Nickelback Might Well be Canada's Most Successful Rock Band," *The Ottawa Citizen*, Ottawa, ON, January 31, 2002.

Wilton, Lisa. "Nickelback Takes Care of Business," *Calgary Sun*, Calgary, AB, February 3, 2000.

OUR LADY PEACE
Articles
Bell, Mike. "Our Lady Peace Redefines Own Sound," *Calgary Sun*, Calgary, AB, September 3, 2005.

Durham, Victoria. "Our Lady Peace—Weight and Bleed," *Rock Sound*, London, November 2002.

FMQB. "Finding Peace: An Up-Close Interview With Our Lady Peace Frontman Raine Maida," *FMQB*, Cherry Hill, NJ, August 19, 2005.

Stevenson, Jane. "Our Lady Peace Building on Fanbase," *The Toronto Sun*, Toronto, ON, January 21, 1997.

Web Articles
Bliss, Karen. "OLP Begins Work on New CD," http://jam.canoe.ca/Music/Lowdown/2004/11/22/pf-726161.html, July 6, 2003.

Oppenheimer, Lem. "Pop Art: Our Lady Peace Walks the Fine Line Between the Concept and the Hook," http://musictoday.com/news/artist/lady.asp, April 2001.

SIMPLE PLAN
Articles
Bennett, J. "The Band You Love to Hate," *Alternative Press Magazine*, Cleveland, OH, February 2004.

SUM 41
Web Articles
Chorney-Booth, Elizabeth. "Sum 41 Banned in Manitoba! Brown Sound Speaks Out!," http://www.chartattack.com/DAMN/2002/11/2608.cfm, November 26, 2002.

Montgomery, James. "Sum 41 on Getting Serious: 'I'd Like to Think That We're Still Goofballs," http://www.mtv.com/news/articles/1492216/20041012/story.jhtml, Oct. 12, 2004.

THE TRAGICALLY HIP
Articles
Wallace, Wendy. "Get Hip: Canada's Hottest Band Celebrates 10 Years Together," *SEE Magazine*, Edmonton, AB, February 16, 1995.

Watkin, Paul. "No Trouble at the Hip House," *Drop-D Magazine*, Vancouver, BC, October 31, 1996.

Web Articles
Sarzyniak, Larry. "Interview," http://www.hiponline.com/artist/music/t/tragically_hip/interview/100334.html, July 15, 2002.

"The Fans Interview The Hip," http://www.canoe.ca/HipLetter/hip_letter1.html, November 5, 1996.

THE TREWS
Articles
Plummer, Sean. "Hardrock Life," *Access Magazine*, Toronto, ON, October/November 2005.

Web Articles
Grandmond, Krys. "The Trews Bring It Home," http://www.soundline.ca/trews.html.

Whibbs, Shannon. "The Trews Give It All They've Got, and More," http://www.chartattack.com/DAMN/2005/12/0208.cfm, December 2, 2005.

STEVE McLEAN

Steve McLean's passion for music has shaped his life. Although he never hit the big time playing the songs, he's programmed it, DJ'ed it, booked it and written about it. He also admits a fondness for karaoke. When he's not immersed in the latest sounds, Steve plays sports from baseball and volleyball to lawn darts and Frisbee caps. He enjoys travelling and has visited about 50 countries around the world. Currently, Steve is the news editor for ChartAttack.com and *Chart* magazine. He has also written for *Billboard*, *RPM*, *Music Business International*, *Music Publisher Canada*, *Canadian Music Network*, *The Record*, and *Sonic* as well as many other newspapers and magazines. He has a Bachelor of Arts in communications from Wilfred Laurier University and a Bachelor of Applied Arts in journalism from Ryerson.